Helping Employees Manage Careers

The Prentice Hall Series on Human Resource Development

R. WAYNE PACE, EDITOR

❦ ❦

PACE, SMITH, AND MILLS *Human Resource Development: The Field*

OTTE AND HUTCHESON *Helping Employees Manage Careers*

HelpingEmployees Manage Careers

❦ ❦

FRED L. OTTE, Ph.D.
GEORGIA STATE UNIVERSITY

PEGGY G. HUTCHESON, Ph.D.
ATLANTA RESOURCE ASSOCIATES

PRENTICE HALL, Englewood Cliffs, New Jersey 07632

Library of Congress Cataloging-in-Publication Data

Otte, Fred L.
Helping employees manage careers / Fred L. Otte, Peggy G. Hutcheson.
p. cm. -- (The Prentice Hall series on human resource development)
Includes bibliographical references and index.
ISBN 0-13-385287-3
1. Career development. 2. Personnel management. I. Hutcheson, Peggy G. II. Title. III. Series.
HF5549.5.C35088 1991
658.3'124—dc20 91-3773
CIP

Acquisitions editor: Alison Reeves
Production editor: Elaine Lynch
Copy editor: Mary Louise Byrd
Cover design: Mike Fender
Prepress buyer: Debra Kesar
Manufacturing buyer: Mary Ann Gloriande
Editorial assistant: Lourdes Brun

A Division of Simon & Schuster
Englewood Cliffs, New Jersey 07632

Printed in the United States of America
2 4 6 8 10 9 7 5 3 1

ISBN 0-13-385287-3

Prentice-Hall International (UK) Limited, *London*
Prentice-Hall of Australia Pty. Limited, *Sydney*
Prentice-Hall Canada Inc., *Toronto*
Prentice-Hall Hispanoamericana, S.A., *Mexico*
Prentice-Hall of India Private Limited, *New Delhi*
Prentice-Hall of Japan, Inc., *Tokyo*
Simon & Schuster Asia Pte. Ltd., *Singapore*
Editora Prentice-Hall do Brasil, Ltda., *Rio de Janeiro*

❦ ❦

Contents

❦ ❦

List of Exhibits

❦ ❦

Editor's Foreword

The Prentice Hall Series on Human Resource Development seeks to define and give direction to the theory and areas of application involved in developing human beings—employees, managers, executives—who work in organizations.

Although the concern for and the practice of human resource development has long had a place in organizations, the systematic formulation of perspectives, views, knowledge, and methods is just now coming into focus.

The prospects, opportunities, and visions of the future are grounded in the dogged yet exciting work of a generation of writers and practitioners who saw very early that organizational competitiveness and productivity are closely tied to employee knowledge, attitudes, and skills.

The content of each volume in this series will focus on a specific role or area of application and will review the theory, principles, research, and skills involved in understanding, appreciating, and performing the role or working in the area.

The books in the HRD series may be used by both practitioners and academicians who have an interest in the field. Since each book has a strong application dimension that is buttressed by theory and research, employees who work in personnel development, management development, employee development, technical development, professional development, sales development, and personal skills development will find each book useful and enlightening.

College and university faculty who prepare students for careers in HRD will discover that the books in this series provide compact and detailed statements of the critical knowledge and competencies that a prospective practitioner needs in order to perform effectively.

Students will recognize that the materials represent real practices in the field, and HRD professionals will recognize that the information and procedures are theoretically sound.

The books in this series may be used as the primary texts in HRD courses in programs such as adult and vocational education, personnel/human resources and industrial relations, behavioral and social sciences, human and educational services, organizational communication and corporate media, and curriculum/instruction and educational psychology.

They may also be used as supplementary textbooks in courses in related programs where students are preparing for careers in training and development. Departments such as communication, organizational/industrial psychology, instructional science, organizational behavior, marketing, and administrative sciences are more and more offering courses that lead to careers in human resource development. These books provide the fundamentals of the field and build very nicely on theoretical foundations in related disciplines.

The books in this series may be used in both undergraduate and dual-level (graduate and undergraduate) courses. They are especially appropriate in courses where working professionals are enrolled. The authors and editors recognize that some courses prepare students in more than one role. The compactness of the books in this series allows them to be mixed and matched to meet the specific needs of HRD students, faculty, and courses.

R. WAYNE PACE

Preface

This book is for three groups of people. Human resources professionals who have been given responsibility for employee career development will find in it practical suggestions for getting started with the most common career development practices. The book has been designed so that the first chapter and any other single chapter can stand alone. Suggestions on where to go for further information are provided, making this book a good starting point for those who are new to the field.

Managers can easily and quickly read all or part of the book to gain an understanding of what needs to be done and why in employee career development. They will then be better equipped to provide resources to whomever is directly supporting employee career development.

Students in higher education who are in human resource development academic preparation programs will gain a picture of the best ways to implement the most common employee career development practices. They will also find suggestions for further study that provide a foundation for critiquing the suggestions for practice that are found here.

The perspective is highly practical; yet the various chapters are held together by a systems orientation for both organizational and individual career development. The opening chapter briefly sets the stage. Although some of the terms and definitions in the first chapter are commonly accepted in the field, the authors themselves work in a way that acknowledges the mythic dimensions of human behavior and the complexities of organizational cultures. This foundation is what gives vitality to the practices that are presented in this book.

❦ ❦

Acknowledgments

We wish to express our appreciation to a number of people who have assisted in very specific ways with making this book what it is. The countless other people who have contributed to our personal and professional lives in ways that made this work possible we acknowledge to ourselves daily and to them individually.

Wayne Pace, the series editor, made us part of this total effort, and we greatly appreciate the invitation he gave us. Wayne also was understanding and helpful throughout the writing and production processes.

Our editors at Prentice Hall and the rest of the staff there gave us what was needed from them quickly and effectively. They were indispensable, of course.

Three highly knowledgeable employee career development experts, Steve Merman, Lynn Slavenski, and Robert Stump, reviewed early plans for the book and sample chapters. Both their theoretical understanding of the field and their extensive hands-on experience were brought to bear in their highly valuable suggestions.

A number of other people provided materials and/or critiqued chapters. The practical orientation and encouragement of these career development professionals were very helpful. We are indebted to Jennifer Bush of The Coca-Cola Company and Isa Williams of C&S/Sovran Financial Corporation for reactions to the chapter on HR staff advising. The career center chapter benefited greatly from ideas and extensive material provided by Nita Vallens.

Almost the entire staff of the Career Development Center at Georgia State University provided reactions to that chapter—Connie Ward, Jennifer Purdon, Cathy Duke, and Eileen Trewartha. Cathy Duke additionally did background research for us. Virginia Berlin of the Internal Revenue Service provided unique reactions to the career center chapter.

Cherrie Kassem carefuly critiqued the writing of the entire manuscript. She offered a multitude of helpful suggestions based on her experience both as a writer and as a career development professional.

John Preston, Chairman of the Department of Vocational and Career Development at Georgia State University, was very supportive of this effort throughout, as was the staff of the department. GSU graduate students read and reacted to preliminary drafts of some chapters. Their warm reception was encouraging.

Sheila Thomas, Nancy Brigman, and Steve Campbell of Atlanta Resource Associates assisted in many ways with details of getting the manuscript ready. We particularly appreciate their consistent emotional support and their patience with our, at times, frantic work pace.

Clients of Atlanta Resource Associates were generous in allowing us to adapt materials that had been developed when working with them.

Some errors will probably remain, despite our best intentions and the help of the many people to give you a perfect book. For the imperfections we are completely responsible and would appreciate your calling them to our attention.

Fred L. Otte
Peggy G. Hutcheson
Atlanta, Georgia

CHAPTER 1

❦ ❦

Getting Started

"I've been asked to head up the Career Development Task Force; and honestly, I don't know where to begin," Jim confided to his friend. "It's beginning to look like a lifetime effort just to decide what programs we need to include. Then we have to figure out how to design all the information and materials we'll need to help our employees manage their careers. I've been reading a lot in order to get some ideas. There is some really good material out there, but it just seems overwhelming."

This book was inspired by the many "Jims" and "Janes" whom we have heard from over the years. It is not designed to cover all the theory that exists on career planning and development. Nor is it designed to provide a comprehensive model for developing career systems that integrate all the human resource practices in an organization. Instead, the purpose of this book is to provide you with methods and materials for the most common practices in employee career development. It will provide real examples of what works, and it will present ways that you can use to structure these components into an overall career system when your organization is ready to take that step.

Many theoretical approaches to career development have already been published. Books on career systems, organizational career development, and especially on approaches to counseling, are readily available. What is not so available, however, are sources of information on applications of the theory and implementations of the systems described in other publications. That is why we wrote this book. We wanted to present practical suggestions from programs that work, idea starters to generate new, successful applications, and an approach that is well grounded, yet leaves room for individual creativity.

Career development has become one of the human resource activities that those entering the work force expect to find in employing organizations. It has become an important aspect of any organization's ability to accomplish its human resource goals, generally described in such terms as "to recruit, retain, and develop quality people to meet the organization's business goals, today and in the future." Career development is no longer on the periphery of an organization's human resource mission. Today people development is one of the most important activities that organizations can invest in to ensure the quality, innovation, and productivity they want from all their employees.

❦ *Value*

Many professionals who are skilled and competent in other areas of human resource development—training, organizational development, staffing—receive assignments in career development. By selecting pertinent sections of this book, these professionals can learn how to apply their existing skills to develop and implement excellent career development programs. They may also discover areas where they may need further assistance, either through researching materials or seeking out experienced professionals. In these pages professionals will find a guide on how to choose among the methods and materials that should be considered as they initiate or change any of the most frequently used career development system components.

Those who receive academic preparation for designing and managing organizational career development programs generally leave programs well grounded in the theory and tradition of organizational career development. Often, however, these programs devote little discussion to how these concepts are most successfully applied in organizations. For this reason this book focuses on applications.

❦ *Chapter Organization*

In this chapter you will find

1. A description of the audience for whom this book is written
2. Definitions of terms common to several career development program components
3. Models to show how these components fit into a career system
4. A general design model for developing any of the components
5. An approach to designing evaluation processes for any of the components
6. A suggested approach for making best use of this book

❦ *Learning Objectives*

After reading this chapter you will be able to

1. Decide if this book is intended for you
2. Understand the meaning of terms commonly used in employee career development
3. Describe at least one approach that enables you to integrate your career development program components into a career system
4. Understand the steps necessary to develop each of the career development components described in other chapters of this book
5. Begin making decisions about the type of evaluation processes that you want to include in your career development program design
6. Identify how this book can be most useful to you

INTENDED AUDIENCE

Helping Employees Manage Careers is for those who have some experience in human resource development but do not have specialized experience in career development. Designing career development programs calls for many of the same competencies needed in other human resource processes. Patricia McLagan has identified 11 roles that a professional must play in developing and maintaining a complete program for organizational career development (1989, 49–59)*. Briefly, these roles and their links with career development design are the following:

Researcher —identifies, develops, or tests new information and uses it in developing or improving the components of career development

Marketer—does all the activities involved with getting others to buy into the viewpoints, programs, and services offered through the career development programs

Organization change agent—influences and supports the changes in organizational behavior (including norms, values, and practices) needed to ensure success of the career development programs

Needs analyst— identifies ideal career-related performance or conditions and compares this ideal with current performance or conditions

Program designer—prepares objectives, defines content, and selects and sequences activities for a specific career development intervention

*From *Models for HRD Practice*, copyright 1989, American Society for Training and Development, Alexandria, Va. Reprinted with permission. All rights reserved.

Materials developer—produces instructional or informational materials to support the career development components

Instructor/facilitator—presents information, directs structured learning experiences, and manages group discussions and group processes for career planning workshops, manager's role workshops, or other learning events needed to implement career development programs

Individual career development advisor—helps individuals assess personal competencies, values, and goals and identify, plan, and implement development and career actions

Administrator—coordinates and supports services for the delivery of career development programs

Evaluator—identifies the impact of the career development program components on individual and/or organization effectiveness

Manager—supports and leads the career development group's work and links that work with the total organization

All of these roles, plus the specialized role of career counselor, are included in our discussion of the major career development components.

How to Use This Book

Some of you may elect to read straight through this book. It is designed, however, to be used somewhat differently. We suggest that everyone read this first chapter. Then, depending on where you are in your career development knowledge and experience and where your organization is in its career development design, you may wish to select from the other chapters those areas that seem to be pertinent for you in designing or upgrading your career development program or offer information on components that you know little about to stimulate your thinking in these areas.

Each component has value. Each component is somewhat independent. Yet each also has an interdependency with the others. Thus; in discussing the components that are widely used in organizational career development, we recognize that the components and their descriptions are not entirely discrete. There is considerable overlap in how some are designed and implemented, one obvious example being the content of career planning workshops and the content of career planning workbooks. Even though the content may be similar, we deal with them independently, because they serve very different purposes with different target groups.

To help you decide where you need to focus your attention, Exhibit 1-1 gives a brief description of the components and the advantages/disadvantages of including each in your employee career development program.

The material in these chapters is the beginning, not the end, of what you need to know to develop and implement successful career development programs. Consider the following:

- How can I keep career development fresh and alive in this organization?
- How can we publicize and market our programs internally?
- What must I do to ensure that the career development interventions are making a difference, not merely existing?
- What changes in the organization create new career development issues that should be addressed in the program components?
- What happens if the sponsor for the initial career development program is no longer here?

Keeping these questions in mind as you make ongoing decisions about career development will help to ensure that your program truly does aid employees to manage their careers.

DEFINITIONS

To enhance your understanding of the discussion, here we define some terms that apply to several, or even all, components.

A person's *career* is a series of work-related positions, paid or nonpaid, that help him or her to grow in job skills, success, and/or fulfillment.

Career development is the lifelong series of activities that contribute to a person's career exploration, establishment, success, and/or fulfillment.

Career planning is a deliberate process through which an individual becomes aware of personal skills, interests, knowledge, motivations, and other characteristics; acquires information about opportunities and choices; identifies career-related goals; and establishes action plans to attain specific goals.

Assessment is a term often associated with career development and planning. *Individual assessment* provides career planners with information and insights about who they are and what they can do well. In *self-assessment*, each participant examines some aspect of self (skills, interests, values) to determine some relative strengths or priorities.

Exhibit 1-1
Descriptions of Career Development Components with Advantages and Disadvantages

Component	Advantages	Disadvantages
Career Planning Workshops	Offer visible, measurable product; can be used to introduce other components.	May create impression that career development is"training,"rather than an overall approach to development.
Career Counseling	Serves to reinforce effectiveness of other components; provides highly professional approach to career development.	Lacks much visibility; may need to overcome impression that career development is for those with problems.
Manager's Role Programs	Reinforce that managers have legitimate roles in employee development; provide skills and information managers need to be effective.	Without supports and training, may result in lowered credibility for career development.
Career Advising	Supports counseling and manager's roles in realistic, cost-effective ways.	Lowered visibility for career assistance.
Career Workbooks	Makes career planning and development readily available to larger groups of employees.	May need support that is not easily obtained by employees not in home office location.
Career Centers	Visible, tangible places to supplement other career activities; central location for information dissemination.	Require some capital expenditures; require ongoing staffing and maintenance.

Assessment by others (managers, peers, etc.) provides individuals with information about the perceptions of those who have information that might be useful to them in planning their careers; and *standardized assessments*, using published instruments or other tools, provide participants with information about how they compare with other people in the areas being measured.

Some commonly used individual assessment instruments or psychological tests include

Intelligence—general learning and problem-solving ability

Aptitude—capacity for learning, usually measured for specific areas such as verbal, mathematical/computation or reasoning, and spatial relations

Personality—behavioral tendencies, such as preferring to respond with thinking as opposed to feeling or to create stability instead of change

Occupational interests—preferences for working in certain types of situations, such as preferring to be outdoors alone instead of selling indoors or to troubleshoot technical equipment instead of doing counseling

Values—what the individual considers important: pay, time for leisure activities, or work that gives a sense of achievement (may be considered one aspect of personality)

Environmental assessment is a second major type of assessment used in career planning. In making an environmental assessment, the career planner gathers data about the world of work—how jobs and organizations are changing, what trends are important for reality-based career planning, and what skills are most prized for today and the future. In addition, he or she obtains information about the company or employing organization—the goals of the business, the different functions within the company and the skills, knowledge and experience important to those different functions, the structure and organization of the company, and trends important to careers. These types of assessment are summarized in Exhibit 1-2.

RELATIONSHIPS WITHIN A CAREER DEVELOPMENT SYSTEM

Each of the components described in this book—career planning workshops or seminars, career counseling, career advising, career planning workbooks, the manager's role in career development, career resource centers—is an element of what may be considered a larger career system. Generally, the term *career system* is used when there is a conscious effort to integrate the different components so that they support each other, overlap is minimized, and there are clear relationships between the components and the information used by individuals and by the organization to make decisions affecting individuals' careers.

Exhibit 1-2
Types of Assessment Summarized

Types of Assessment	
Individual	**Environmental**
Self Assessment	Data about the World of Work
Assessment by Others	Information about Your Organization
Standardized Assessment	Trends

Exhibit 1-3
Organizational Career Cycle

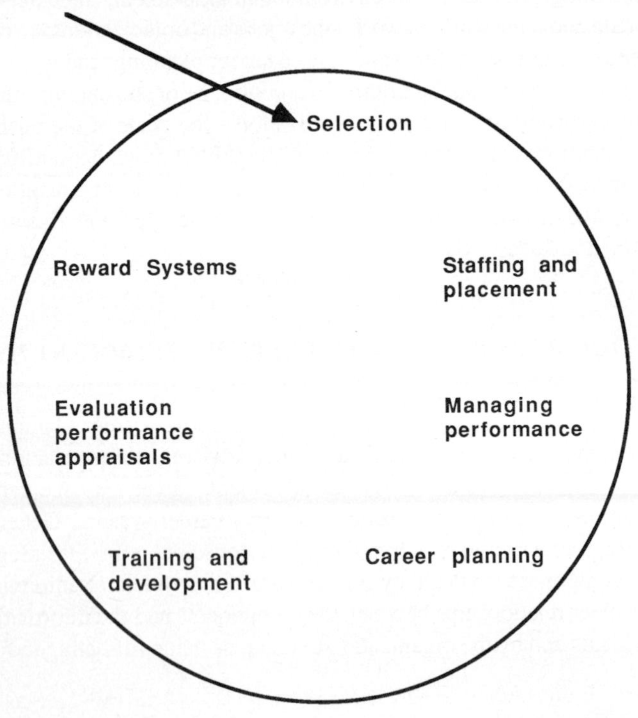

Viewing career development in its broadest sense, we might say that every activity within the organization that has impact on an individual's current or future work options is included in the career system. Exhibit 1-3 is one model for how this approach to designing an organizational career system might look. Note, however, that every human resource activity can be carried out without a career development focus (traditional approach) or it can include a career development focus. Exhibit 1-4 contrasts the two approaches.

Other strategies for describing career systems depict each of the career development program components, showing how each serves as an *input* (i.e., provides information or preparation) either for other career development components or for the organization's staffing or development information systems. In these career systems the *outputs* are decisions made by the individual, the organization, or both regarding the individual's work assignments and/or development.

Keep in mind, as you use the information in this book, that the impact of any one component may be magnified many times when a systems view is taken to designing the component and linking it with other (presently existing or future) components. There is even a danger that career planning and development activities may be seen from a personal perspective as useful, but largely futile, enterprises if some attempt is not made to link these activities with organizational decision processes.

Designing Career Development Components

Specific information about the design of each component in this book is given in the chapter devoted to that component. This section provides an overall approach to design—the broader, more conceptual model into which the specific suggestions in the following chapters may fit.

❦ *Design Step 1: Needs Analysis*

Before you make any decision about a component, and certainly before you design any materials, you must conduct some form of needs analysis. This front-end analysis should be done to help decide whether something is even needed and then to decide how that identified need might best be filled. Needs analysis may be very formal. Often career development needs are gleaned from specific items in an organizational climate or effectiveness survey. They may be identified by examining some very specific indicators that employee development and retention goals are not being met; turnover rate, information gained during exit interviews, recruiting expenses, and depth charts are some examples.

Exhibit 1-4
Traditional versus Career Development Focus

Activity	Traditional Focus	Career Development Focus
Human resource planning	Analyzes jobs, skills, tasks-present and future. Projects needs. Uses statistical data.	Adds information about individual interests, preference, and the like to data. Provides career path information.
Training and development	Provides opportunities for learning skills, information, and attitudes related to job.	Adds individual growth or "training by objectives orientation."
Performance appraisal	Rating and/or rewards.	Adds development plans and individual goal setting.
Recruiting and placement	Matching organization's needs with qualified individuals.	Matching individual and jobs based on a number of variables.
Compensation and benefits	Rewards for time, productivity, talent, and so on.	Adds non-job-related activities.

Conducting a survey specifically for career-related issues is another way to ascertain needs.

One effective way to develop a needs assessment process is to begin with rather informal discussions to identify the general themes about which you need more information. If people in the organization have indicated that they want career development programs in addition to what the company already offers, ask them to identify just what they see as the need behind their suggestion. Once you have identified some issues, make a brief survey to see whether others agree that these are the issues. A "gap analysis" is one tool that may point up both your strengths in developing people and the opportunities you have for adding other career assistance. Exhibit 1-5 shows some sample items from a gap analysis.

Regardless of how formal or informal your needs assessment is, be sure that it includes some information about the indicators of success important to those in the organization whose support you need. For example, if your CEO is interested in career development to develop cross-training among the technical ranks, you need to know this. If the human resources director is interested in reducing the number of experienced hires made each year, or if the manager of manufacturing operations wants to keep people on the job for at least 18 months, or if the employees want access to information about vacancies throughout the organization, your program goals need to take all of these interests into consideration.

Exhibit 1-5
Sample Gap-Analysis Survey

Career Development Survey

Read each item in the center of the page. Then mark in the section to the left of the item the degree to which you believe the company is providing the service, information, or opportunities described. Next, mark in the section to the right of the item the degree to which you believe the item needs to be offered to meet the career development needs of employees.

1 2 3 4 5	1. Information about work in all areas of the company.	1 2 3 4 5
1 2 3 4 5	2. Open information about what is needed in order to be promoted to a higher level.	1 2 3 4 5
1 2 3 4 5	3. Opportunities to develop my technical skills.	1 2 3 4 5

❦ *Design Step 2: Determining Objectives*

The program objectives that you establish for career development draw directly on those identified in your needs assessment. Such objectives may be both quantitative and qualitative. Quantitative objectives describe such things as how much, how often, or how many. Sample quantitative objectives might be to conduct 10 career planning seminars, including at least 15 field engineers, or to publish a career planning workbook that results in career plans being filed for 100 staff support personnel or to reduce turnover among systems analysts to be in line with industry standard rates. *Qualitative objectives* describe how well or to what standards you want something done. Sample qualitative objectives might be for managers and employees to report that their career discussions were productive and satisfying, or for employees to report that the career center is attractive and easy to use.

❦ *Design Step 3: Developing the Component*

The criteria for developing the component result from the first two design steps. Here, you must examine the alternatives for designing the component and then make decisions that will help you meet your goals. Keep in mind that even though there may be an optimal design for your organization, it is unlikely that there is a single "best" or effective way to design any component. The "best" design is the one that meets the real needs of the group you want to serve, accommodates the goals you have established, and accomplishes all this within the norms and expectations of your organization and within your budget.

Exhibit 1-6
Types of Evaluation Data

If you want to know:	Try these methods:
What do participants enjoy most/least about the workshop?	Feedback survey at the end of the program Post - workshop interviews
What did participants learn?	Skills checks Pre - and post - surveys on content of workshop Examining documents indicating use of skills (e.g., job applications)
Did participants behavior change as a result of the program?	Interviews or surveys with others (e.g., managers, coworkers, employees) Tracking organizational information (e.g., number of lateral transfers, turnover data, enrichment activities)
Did it make a difference?	Organization surveys, opinion surveys, job satisfaction surveys, productivity data, exit interviews

This material adapted from a model developed by Dr. Donald Kirkpatrick and used with permission.

❦ *Design Step 4: Testing the Component*

One often overlooked element in developing a career development component is the field test. Before any component is introduced on a large scale, it should be tested on a sample of the actual group it is designed to serve. Even though you may not be able to test the long-range effectiveness of the component in such a pilot test, you will gain invaluable information about what works well and what improvements you need to consider.

❦ *Design Step 5: Evaluating the Component*

Evaluation is often described by types or levels of evaluation: reaction (Did they like it?), learning (Did they get it?), behavior change (Did they do anything differently?), and results (Did it make a difference?). For a summary of ideas on useful types of data, see Exhibit 1-6.

There is one basic rule for evaluation: Select those evaluation tools and processes that answer the questions you and other decision makers need answered in order to make decisions about the career development program in your organization.

CHAPTER 2

❦ ❦

Career Planning Workshops and Seminars

At the first meeting of the Career Development Task Force, members of the group begin to talk about the goals of their project. Before long, Jesse, supervisor of the accounting department, says, "What we need around here is a good career planning workshop. My friend at Micro Company says their workshop is really powerful." "I agree," interjects Susan, from data processing. "We need something that will serve as our flagship, a product that will show people that we are getting things done."

Most people have seen or heard of career planning workshops, so most who are asked to design a career-related program think of these workshops as one of the first pieces in their career program.

❦ *Value*

Career planning workshops are the most visible and among the most widely used career development programs in organizations. They are valuable for the learning they provide and for the links they offer with other parts of the career development system. Workshops are concrete "products" in the career system. Having products is extremely important in organizations in which managers are accustomed to looking for results in terms of how many and how often. Unfortunately, many career planning workshops are decided upon with little more thought than that given by the task force in the scenario just described. This chapter will help you think, plan, and design your workshop in a more systematic way.

❦ *Chapter Organization and Objectives*

In this chapter you will find

1. Definitions for terms used in career planning workshops
2. An overview of career planning workshops
3. A description of how these workshops fit into the larger career development system
4. A discussion of decisions you will need to make as you design your workshop
5. Sample agendas from actual workshops
6. Methods and materials for designing workshop modules for nine topics commonly found in career planning workshops
7. Evaluation techniques
8. Resources for further study

❦ *Learning Objectives*

In this chapter you will learn design processes that lead to successful workshops, typical content areas for career planning workshops, and evaluation techniques for tracking results of these programs. You will also find samples of agendas from effective workshops, as well as samples of materials used in each of the typical major content areas. After reading this chapter you will be able to

1. Identify the decisions you must make to design a career planning workshop
2. Describe the major content areas of career planning workshops
3. Begin to select methods that support the goals of your career planning program
4. Design evaluation processes to help you track the effectiveness of your program in order to provide the information your decision makers want

DEFINITIONS

Before you read farther, review the section on definitions in Chapter 1. All of the terms there are pertinent to career planning workshops. A couple of other terms need some clarification and are discussed here.

In organizations, employee career planning is most often facilitated through workshops or seminars. The term *workshop* usually implies a planned learning event in which participants are expected to be actively involved, completing exercises and inventories and participating in skills practice sessions. A *semi-*

nar, on the other hand, is most often associated with the opportunity to share ideas with peers and, perhaps, "experts" on the subject at hand, with discussion groups, panels, and question-and-answer periods as the primary learning vehicles. The distinction between workshops and seminars is often blurred in practice, and most career planning events are actually combinations of the two formats.

OVERVIEW

Organizations reputed to have outstanding career development systems offer career planning workshops and seminars more frequently than any other type of career service (Gutteridge and Otte 1983). Even though the many aspects of career planning programs differ from organization to organization, one thing that organizations offering such workshops share is a common set of beliefs supporting career planning. These beliefs include the following:

- Individuals are responsible for their own career growth and development.
- Current information about self (including how others see you), about the organization, and about options leads to more realistic goals and more effective decision making.
- The organization is responsible for creating an environment that allows individual growth and for making information available about the company's philosophies, policies, and work options.
- Managers play important roles in supporting and facilitating employee career development.
- Growth begins on the current job assignment.
- Employees should examine a variety of options in managing their careers (developing on the job, moving laterally, moving to a related function or department) other than traditional promotion.
- Skills can be developed to make everyone more effective in personal career management.

Because different organizations have different cultures and needs, career planning workshops differ in goals, content, and methods. If there is such a thing as a "typical" career planning workshop, it probably has these characteristics:

- Lasts for two to three days
- Offered on company time
- Has from 10 to 20 participants

- Led by a training specialist from the company or "team taught" by an external career development consultant and an internal trainer
- Voluntary participation
- Leads to the development of a career plan document

The typical participant is a professional, managerial, or technical employee, most often one who works in the headquarters or in a division located near the main office. This person is participating in career planning in order to obtain a greater sense of direction and more information about careers in the company, rather than to deal with a specific current career problem.

CAREER WORKSHOPS AND SEMINARS IN THE LARGER CAREER DEVELOPMENT SYSTEM

Organizations that take a systematic view of career development often give significance to the career planning workshop (see Exhibit 2-1). The workshop is a primary vehicle for disseminating information about the system. Often, a segment of the program is devoted to an explanation of the system, a discussion with executives about its implementation, and descriptions of resources offered through the system.

Each of the major career development programs that organizations offer is linked or related to the career planning workshop. Career discussions with managers often are "next steps" after the career planning workshop. Career counseling or advising may precede the workshop. This counseling may be used to screen and select appropriate participants for the program. In addition, counseling or advising often follows a workshop for employees who have special career needs.

Career workbooks are frequently used as preparation, allowing employees to complete a number of assessments and activities before attending a workshop. In these cases, the pre-work serves as a test of commitment, answering the question "Is the employee willing to exert the energy and spend the time required for career planning?" The pre-work also allows time-consuming inventories to be completed outside the group, thus optimizing the use of group time.

Career planning workshops may be held in a conference room in the career resource center. If space does not permit the program to be run from such a resource center, participants may be given printed material describing the information available in the center or they may spend time doing research in the resource center during the career planning workshop.

Exhibit 2-1
Career Planning Model

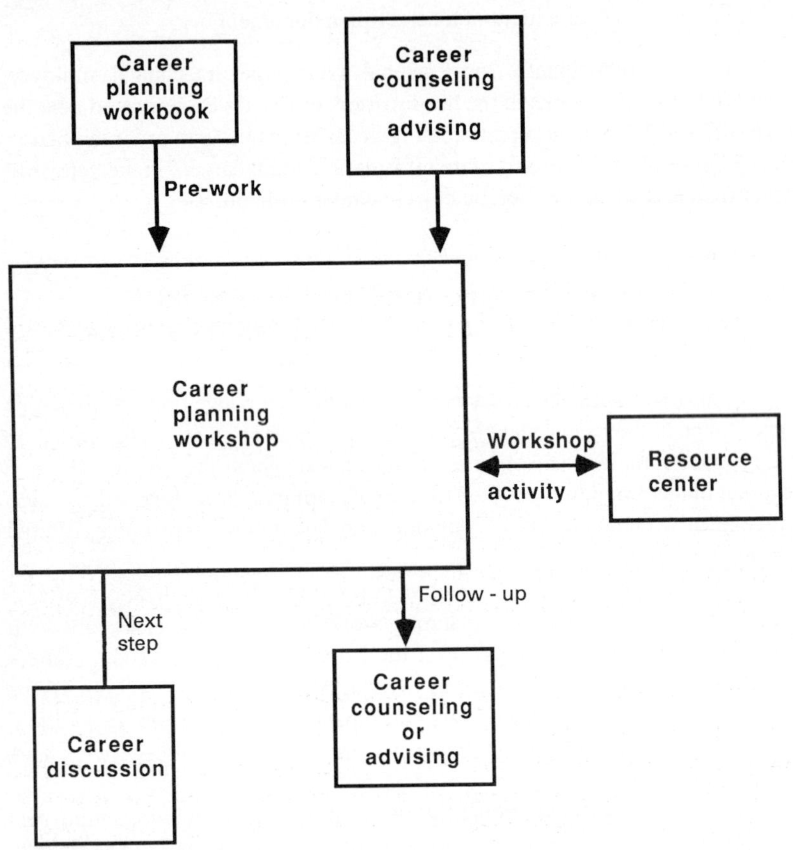

DECISIONS TO MAKE IN DESIGNING CAREER PLANNING WORKSHOPS AND SEMINARS

You must make numerous choices that you must make as you design a career planning workshop or seminar. Each of these choices influences how others perceive the program and (potentially) the effectiveness of the program. The following discusses some of the issues you should consider.

How visible will the workshop or seminar be? Will the workshop be widely announced or quietly promoted? Would you rather have a waiting list that will take you a year to work through or be able to accommodate quickly those who hear of the program and wish to participate? To answer these questions requires that you examine how strongly the program is supported. Long-term commitments to career planning indicate more visibility. Less commitment from senior management may call for an approach that will not raise expectations that cannot be met. Answers to this issue also require that you have an approved implementation plan, including instructor time and budget.

How will we "package" the program? Whether you decide to make your own or to purchase program materials, and whether you decide to design and facilitate the workshop yourself or to bring in someone with special expertise to assist you, should be decisions that reflect your organization's culture, as well as your budget and timetable. It is important to develop culturally consistent and highly credible products if the program is to have maximum impact. For example, if your company normally provides training programs that include videotapes, slide-sound presentations, and well-packaged participant materials, you will certainly not want to use only a flip chart and participant materials with no visual impact. If your organization typically brings in outside experts to lead programs or consult on new program designs, your career planning program will carry more weight in the organization if you also make use of these resources.

Who will deliver, or present, the program? Excellent presentation and facilitation skills are called for in the primary instructor's role for presenting career planning workshops. Since career planning requires a great deal of personal introspection and analysis, someone who has counseling, as well as training, skills is an excellent choice. In addition to the primary facilitator(s) for this program, you may wish to involve others whose participation can give stature or add important information. Having a senior executive open the program is often a powerful strategy. Including managers or employees representing a variety of work functions as resource persons, or having them present a panel discussion of opportunities in the business, can add information and credibility.

Although career planning workshops and seminars vary considerably in their content and methods, virtually all share the following elements: individual assessment (information about self), environmental assessment (information about work), comparison of self-perceptions with those of others (reality testing), establishing long- and short-term goals (goal setting), choosing among alternatives (decision making), and establishing and implementing the plan (action planning). These factors are depicted in Exhibit 2-2.

CAREER PLANNING WORKSHOP AGENDA

How the content of a career planning workshop is organized and presented certainly differs from program to program. We present some sample agendas (Exhibits 2-3 and 2-4) to help you see how the specific topics are ordered and what time frames may be allotted to them. As you examine the agendas, notice these characteristics:

- Time is allotted early in the programs to understanding concepts and likely/unlikely outcomes of planning one's career.
- Self-assessment is an important aspect of all programs.
- Information about the organization is included.
- Participants are asked to create a career plan so that they leave with a product from the workshops.
- In three-day programs, more time is spent on assessment, and an entire day is devoted to developing the plan and strategies for implementing the plan.

In the design of your program, be sure that the needs assessment data you collected from your clients, customers, and potential participants are clearly reflected in the time allowed for different workshop segments. For example, if the data indicate a general lack of information about the company, its goals, and opportunities, expand this section and enrich it with media, guest speakers, and in-depth discussions. If your data show poor skills in making decisions or implementation of plans, then place proportionately more emphasis on these aspects.

Now that we have examined the overall structure of career planning workshops, let's look at the strategies used in conducting the workshops. The remainder of this chapter describes methods and materials for each section of a career planning workshop or seminar. This information will provide you with options and resources for developing your own learning activities.

Exhibit 2-2
Career Planning Model

Information about self	To plan your career you need to have clear and specific information about your skills, interests, work values, and motivations. This area will help you examine past experiences as a basis for identifying the most important ingredients for your personal growth and future success.
Information about work	Different work options provide different challenges and payoffs. This section helps you look at the job opportunities within the company to discover which assignments might offer you learning, variety, and career growth.
Reality testing	It is important to know how others see you, your skills, knowledge, and career accomplishments. It is also important to know how they view work options within the company. Also, you will examine others' perceptions of you and use this information in your career decisions.
Goal setting	Career plans should be based on long-term goals that are exciting, meaningful, and realistic. In this section you will look into your future to identify those ingredients important to your sense of success.
Decision making	Almost every day you make choices that influence your careers. Finding ways to make better decisions based on your goals is an important step for managing careers effectively.
Action planning	The most important step in career planning involves turning our plans and dreams into positive action steps. In this step you will develop plans to translate your goals to concrete actions. Careers grow inch by inch, rather than in major leaps. Before your career planning process is complete, you will have a detailed plan for what to do next.

Exhibit 2-3
Sample Agenda—Two-Day Career Planning Workshop

Before the program–Two weeks prior to the workshop participants receive a letter confirming their participation in the program and package of work to be completed before coming to the workshop. The exercises in this package include skills inventory, values identification, life accomplishments inventory, and a reading describing career direction options.

Day 1

8:30–10:00 **Introduction and Overview of Career Planning**

Welcome and Introduction to Program

Welcome by general manager
Overview of agenda and outcomes
Participant Introductions (Statements of expectations for the program)

Overview of Career Development

Company's philosophy
Why career planning is needed
What career planning is and is not
Career planning model

10:00–Noon **Self - Assessment: Part 1**

Individual Self - Assessment: Values

Values card sort exercise
Reconciling with values pre-worl
Introduce career planning summary work sheet

Individual Self - Assessment: Skills

Motivated skills exercise
Examining life accomplishments (synthesize exercise with pre-work)
Identifying accomplishment themes
Preferred work skills (from pre-work inventory)
Fill in career planning summary work sheet

1:00–3:30 **Self Assessment: Part 2**

Individual Self - Assessment: Career Anchors

Career anchoring pattern exercise
Small group discussions
Fill in career planning summary work sheet

Individual Self - Assessment: Preferences

What success means to me
Skills, knowledge, personal qualities
Fill in career planning summary work sheet

Individual Self - Assessment: Career Path Pattern

Synthesize with direction options from pre-work
Fill in career planning summary work sheet

3:30–4:30 **Environmental Assessment**

Information About the Company

Goals, growth areas, expectations, turnover, competition for jobs, skills for the future
Fill in career planning summary work sheet

Personal career profile

Reality test how you see self at this point by sharing in group

Day 2

8:30–10:00 Goal Setting

Warm - Up Exercise

Review of where we've been and where we're going

Setting goals–where do I want to be?

Creating an ideal future

Future skills and accomplishments
Desired lifestyle
Life and career goals

10:15–1:30 Environmental Assessment: Part 2

Career resources in the company

Introduce support services and hand out information

Marketing yourself–what it takes to achieve your goals here

Describe resource people who will be with the group for lunch and brainstorm questions/issues to be discussed

Lunch with resource people

Review lunch discussions

1:30–4:30 DEVELOPING CAREER ACTION PLANS

Making Career Decisions

Identifying long-range alternatives
Identifying short-range alternatives

Improving career decisions

Decision styles and ways to enhance them

Creating your career plan

Reconciling your goals with options
Next career steps
Development action plan
Contingency planning

Making It Happen–Making Commitments to Next Steps

Summary and Adjourn

TECHNIQUES AND MATERIALS FOR CAREER PLANNING WORKSHOPS AND SEMINARS

❦ *Before the Workshop*

Before the workshop, one issue is whether or not to send materials to participants to complete before they attend. The decision is not an easy one. Distributing a package of information and exercises for completion before the workshop can streamline the workshop, allowing you to spend class time on activities better suited to groups. Other advantages of sending materials ahead of time are that it allows participants to complete these exercises at their own

Exhibit 2-4
Sample Agenda—Three-Day Career Planning Workshop

Day 1

9:00 –12 Noon **Overview of Career Development**

1. Participant introductions
2. Sharing of expectations
3. Overview of career development/career planning process
4. Discussion of why career planning is needed
5. Review of program content and objectives
6. Introduction to organization's career philosophy

1:00–5:00 **Initial Self- Assessment**

1. Who am I? What do I want to do?

Self-concept, values clarification, personality characteristics/personal style, motivational patterns, occupational interests, personal preferences

2. Where have I been?

Personal/educational background, work history and experience, key accomplishments/successes, peak experiences, significant life decisions, satisfying/dissatisfying experiences

Day 2

9 a.m–12 Noon **Completion of Self-Assessment**

1. Where am I now? What can I do?

Analysis of current job (behavior demands, importance of various job elements, likes/dislikes); valued skills and abilities; special knowledge/capabilities; personal qualities; developmental needs; sources of satisfaction/dissatisfaction

2. Where do I want to be?

Occupational daydreams/ideal job description, desired future accomplishments; preferred working environment; ideal life style; career goals; personal goals

1:00–5:00 **Environmental Assessment**

What's out there?

Organization profile/business outlook; opportunity structure/job requirements/selection standards; available career paths/ career options; developmental policies/practices/systems; additional resources and information sources

Day 3

9:00–12 Noon **Integration, Goal Development, and Action Planning**

What's the next step?

Reconciling self-assessment with environmental assessment; identifying long-range alternatives; specifying short-range goals; establishing next career step/setting priorities; preparing developmental action plan; contingency planning.

1:00–5:00 **Designing Implementation Tactics**

How do I get there?
Techniques for marketing yourself; establishing career action projects with time frame for completion; review progress and revise as needed.

Adapted from Thomas G. Gutteridge and Fred L. Otte, *Organizational Career Development: State of thePractice*, Alexandria, Va., ASTD Press, 1983.

---

pace, without concern for being faster or slower than others, and it provides opportunities for participants to get input from others whose opinions they value and who will not be in the workshop (friends, spouse, managers). The disadvantages include the potential for confusing participants or overwhelming them, having some come to the program without completing the assignments, or asking overly busy people to add this work to an already full schedule.

Before you opt to have pre-workshop assignments, consider these:

- How much do the participants travel? Will they be likely to receive the materials in time to complete them?
- Does the culture of the organization support this kind of activity? Do we ask people to do things on their own time and expect them to be done?
- What happens in the program if a significant number of people do not complete the exercises?

If the answers to these questions are positive, then chances are good that pre-work will contribute positively to the workshop. If you do decide on pre-work, be sure that all instructions are clear and that the total amount of time you ask participants to invest is reasonable (usually two hours or less). When you design interesting, thought-provoking pre-work, you provide the mindset that career planning deserves thoughtful consideration and that it can be fun.

❦ *Beginning the Workshop*

How you open the career planning workshop is extremely important. The introduction and beginning exercises set the tone for the entire program. You want to project an image that is a combination of warmth and action-orientation. This section describes some activities that set the stage for an excellent workshop.

If an executive is available to open the program, this endorsement may add to the sense of purpose. You should plan to work with the executive aheadof time, making sure that he or she is totally familiar with the program. You may even wish to suggest what points you would like the executive to cover. Examples of the content of this presentation include how developing people fits into the overall goals of the organization, the company's philosophy or value statements that support career development, and the personal commitments of this executive in supporting career planning and development.

Be sure to cover the outcomes and general flow of the agenda fairly early in the opening. Notice the prominence of these items in both the two-day and the three-day agendas in Exhibits 2-3 and 2-4. These items, and any "housekeeping" items (e.g., how messages are handled), will give everyone a sense of security—they will know what to expect.

Another important aspect of opening the workshop is participant introductions. The introduction process should include information that is relevant to career planning. In programs we have observed, participants share such information as current job title, brief history of positions held in the organization, time in the organization, time on the current job, challenges or rewards of their current work assignments, personal data, statements or analogies describing their current career situations, and expectations of the program. Ask for information that is interesting and relevant but not so much information that introductions are longer than a minute or so per person. Long introductions help group members to get to know each other, but they also delay the proceedings. Participants want to get on with the program.

In a large group, you may wish to have more introductory information shared in small groups, with only key data shared with the total group. If you elect this option, be sure that you allow time for introductions each time participants work with new small groups.

One critical piece of information from participants that you need early in the program is a statement of their expectations. If this is not collected from them before they arrive at the workshop, you need to include a process to get this information in this first section of the program. You can do this as one item of information in their individual introductions or you can ask small groups to describe their expectations for the program. It is important that unrealistic expectations (e.g., that you will have jobs to offer them) or person-specific questions (e.g., what will my benefits be if I choose to take an early retirement?) be tactfully, but firmly, confronted early on. Ask those persons with very specific, personal issues to talk with you at break about other resources that may help them. They can then make an informed decision about whether continuing with the workshop will be a good investment of their time and energy.

Career Development and Career Planning Concepts

Laying the groundwork for a successful workshop or seminar includes some time spent clarifying the terms and concepts that are involved in career planning. If you have sufficient time, this is also a good opportunity to address fears about career planning. You can elicit these fears by having group members identify benefits and risks for career planning, as they see them. Information about the roles for the organization, the individual's manager, and the individual in the career development process may also be explored in this section. Sometimes this is done participatively, with small groups developing their lists; other times a list is distributed to reflect the philosophy of the company concerning roles and responsibilities in career and employee development. Exhibit 2-5 provides typical descriptions of the benefits and risks in career planning.

Charts or models that show the relationship of career planning to other human resource processes and programs may be helpful. A sample is shown in Exhibit 2-6. Pay careful attention to providing enough foundation for your participants without burdening them with unnecessary theory.

Individual Assessments

Most career planning workshops devote considerable time to helping individuals gather data about themselves and to organize that data in ways that enable them to answer the questions of who am I, what can I do, and what do I want to do. Effective career plans are built around the unique skills, experiences, personal qualities, and preferences of individuals. Career planners need concrete, specific information about themselves. Individual assessment exercises and inventories provide information that participants draw on to develop their goal statements and their career plans later in the program.

Many individual assessment exercises are self-assessments. These provide opportunities for participants to appraise themselves in such areas as specific job skills, career and life management skills, life and career values, preferences, occupational interests, success experiences, and perceived needs and weaknesses. Often, assessments include a number of instruments designed and produced by the workshop developers especially for that program. These may consist of a series of open-ended questions, such as those in the life values exercise in Exhibit 2-7. Others are more structured, such as the sample skills inventory in Exhibit 2-8.

In addition to in-house instruments, many career planning workshops use commercially available assessments. These instruments are widely available and appraise skills, values, personality traits, aptitudes, occupational interests, and the like. Workshop leaders report that participants enjoy having some

Exhibit 2-5
Benefits and Risks om Career Planning

	Benefits	Risks
You	❍ More self-determination ❍ More sense of growth ❍ Better fit with job ❍ Better skills in marketing self in career ❍ Less stress from feeling out of control ❍ Improved relationships	❍ Getting unbalanced in direction of self - interests ❍ Feeling overwhelmed with the options available ❍ Stress from decisions involved with making changes ❍ Stress from frustrations of limitations ❍ Fear of discovering incompetence or "bad motives" ❍ Having to change or give up "dreams" ❍ Stress from bringing role conflicts to the surface ❍ Stress from impatience with the status quo
Manager	❍ Having a safe way of letting employees know you care about them as people ❍ Discovering that many fears about employees have no basis in reality; joy in being able to trust them ❍ Having your unit get its job done–well! ❍ Finding that your employees also care about you as a person	❍ Being perceived by employees as less than perfect, weak or soft ❍ Stress from change ❍ Confrontations as conflicts are brought to the surface ❍ Feeling that the job will not get done if time is taken with employees ❍ Having a sense of failure when the process does not work well with certain employees
Organization	❍ Better use of human resources ❍ Productivity improvements in quantity and quality ❍ Organizational adaptability ❍ Employee commitment ❍ Less turnover, absenteeism, tardiness, etc. ❍ Better compliance with legal requirements ❍ Fewer grievances ❍ Better morale ❍ More teamwork spirit ❍ Employee responsibility for self-development	❍ Unmet employee expectations ❍ People overdeveloped for current jobs ❍ Too much emphasis on life planning and not enough on current job performance planning ❍ Initially, more conflict of individuals and organization ❍ Undesirable turnover or too much mobility ❍ Destructive employee competition ❍ Reverse discrimination

commercial instruments interspersed with those developed in-house. Some of the commercial instruments reported as useful by workshop developers and facilitators are listed in Exhibit 2-9. This list is intended to be illustrative, not

Exhibit 2-6
Relationship of Career Planning and Other Human Resources Processes

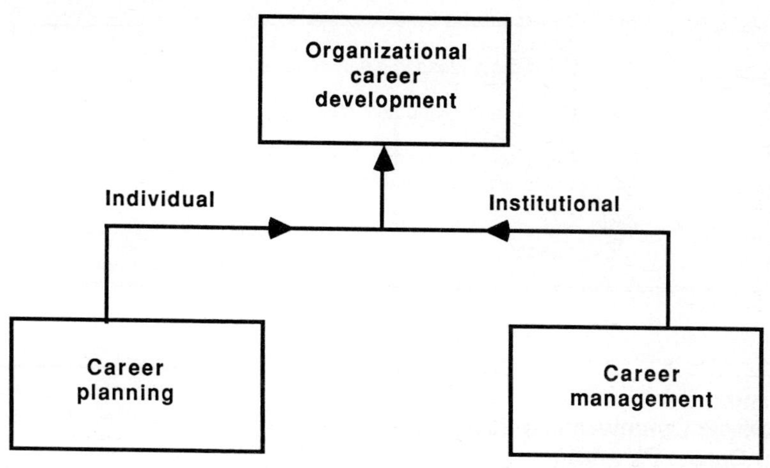

Exhibit 2-7
Sample Life Values Exercise

2. I feel best at work when...
3. When I'm not at work, the things I enjoy most are...
4. I have dreamed of becoming...

---

comprehensive. Further, it is not an endorsement of the instruments, but rather a list of those that we are familiar with through our work and through reports of colleagues.

An "observer" instrument completed by the participants' managers, colleagues, or others who know them well is a technique aimed at giving a reality check to information contributed by individuals. Skills inventories are especially suited to this additional input.

Exhibit 2-8
Sample Skills Inventory

_____	24.	Writing effective memos, letters, and reports	_____
_____	25.	Expressing ideas in clear, coherent ways	_____
_____	26.	Getting and giving accurate information	_____
_____	27.	Being open to feedback from others	_____
_____	28.	Using feedback for improved performance	_____
_____	29.	Staying closely in tune with customer needs	_____

Exhibit 2-9
Sample Commercial Instruments for Career Planning

Career Anchoring Pattern	We know of two instruments that assess this concept, one available through Sources, Inc. (Atlanta, Ga.), and one from University Associates (La Jolla, Calif.).
Management Effectiveness Analysis	Contact Management Research Group (Portland, Maine) for the representative nearest you.
Myers-Briggs Type Indicator	Available from Consulting Psychologist Press (Palo Alto, Calif.) or Educational Testing Service (Princeton, N.J.).
Personal Skills Map	Available from Life Skills Center (Corpus Christi, Tex.) or Atlanta Resource Associates (Atlanta, Ga.).
Self Directed Search	Available from Consulting Psychologist Press (Palo Alto, Calif.).
Strong-Campbell Interest Inventory	Available from Consulting Psychologist Press (Palo Alto, Calif.).
Work Analysis Questionnaire	Available from McBer (Boston, Mass/).

As you develop the assessment portion of the workshop, it is important that you be aware of the need to vary paper-and-pencil instruments and exercises with other forms of activity. Here are some ideas for accomplishing this:

- Develop or purchase a card sort activity to prioritize values, skills, or personal characteristics.
- Create interview exercises for motivated skills, success experiences, or work preferences.
- Computerize your assessments if your participants have skills in using a personal computer and if you have resources to do this.

Also, be aware of the different time frames within which your participants are likely to complete exercises. Often, one or more very analytical individuals slows the pace for others in the group. Planning the program so that instruments are completed just before breaks or lunchtime can help keep the group together without anyone having to wait very long for others to finish.

Still another aspect of some very successful career planning programs is the career planning summary work sheet. This document is used to collect or summarize key data from each of the assessment exercises completed. The summary provides an easy reference for the goal-setting and decision-making sections of the program and is a "product" that gives participants a sense of progress as they move through the workshop. See Exhibit 2-10 for a sample summary page.

Types of Assessment and Sources of Data

We have referred to a number of assessments. Even though you are not likely to use every type, the following lists may be helpful when you begin to make choices about the kinds of assessments to include in your workshop or seminar.

Types of skills and sources of data

1. Organization- or function-specific inventories of skills needed for work in the company

   Developed from job descriptions, selection criteria lists, and/or performance measures; tests developed by professional associations or licensing/certification agencies to test for specialized proficiencies

2. Life and career management skills

   Purchased instruments or developed from "preferred traits" and self-management skills desired in the organization

3. Transferable (functional) skills

Exhibit 2-10
Sample Summary Page

Most Important Work Values

1.
2.
3.
4.
5.

Success

Career Anchors

Important Skills

Skill Strengths	Skills to Develop
1.	1.
2.	2.
3.	3.
4.	4.
5.	5.

Skills for the Future

Skill Strengths	Skills to Develop
1.	1.
2.	2.
3.	3.

Strategies for Skill Development

Lists in publications such as *What Color Is Your Parachute*; synthesis of "most valued" or most widely used skills in your company

4. Management skills

   Published management inventories; instruments developed in-house

5. Preferred skills

   Combination of skills from one of the categories above with a ranking of personal preferences or desire to use the skill

Sources of data on job knowledge

"Preferred experience" or content explanations of job descriptions; functional names of work groups (e.g., purchasing, public relations, mortgage lending)

Types of personality dimensions and sources of data

1. Occupational interests

   Standardized occupational interest inventory (e.g., *Strong-Campbell Interest Inventory* or Holland's *Self-Directed Search*); in-house developed survey; card game or card sort

2. Career anchors

   Published instruments

3. Life values

   Purchased instruments; open-ended exercise; in-house inventory

4. Work values

   Card sort (purchased or developed in-house); inventory (purchased or developed in house)

5. Life stages and needs

   Purchased inventories or those developed from the work of D. Super, D. Levinson, E. Erikson, G. Sheehy, and so on.

6. Motivations

   Interview assessments (e.g., *SIMA* developed by A. Miller); standardized assessments (note: may need psychologist for interpretation); in-house developed instruments

7. Personality/Personal Traits

   Standardized instruments (e.g., *Myers/Briggs Type Indicator* or *Test of Imagination*); most of these require special training for administration and interpretation

❦ *Understanding Work*

No matter how good the assessment processes are, the success of the program is likely to rest on how well you assist participants in analyzing this information in the context of work and of the work options that are available to them. This process is often referred to as "environmental assessment." Through concrete information about the characteristics of various forms of work, specifics on current and potential availability of jobs in areas of interest, and the examination of paths that may lead to desired jobs, career planning becomes a useful tool for your participants. Without this application, assessment activities are merely a nice adventure. Most people enjoy knowing themselves better, but few are able to take the information and make concrete applications without assistance. Completing this section of the career planning workshop should allow participants to identify realistic career options that appeal to them.

Exhibit 2-11
Career Patterns

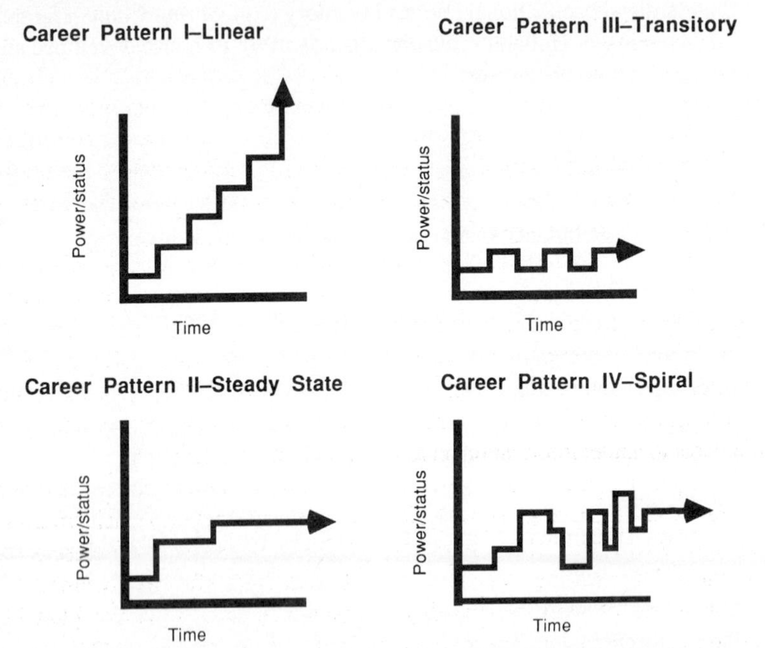

Michael J. Driver, "Career Concepts and Career Management in Organizations" in BEHAVIORAL PROBLEMS IN ORGANIZATIONS edited by Cary L. Cooper, copyright 1979, pp. 79-139. Adapted by permission of Prentice-Hall, Inc., Englewood Cliffs, NJ.

Understanding work usually begins with understanding the structure of work options. The desired outcome of this section is to have participants recognize the payoffs that are associated with different approaches to developing their careers. Presenting information or planning exercises on options helps participants do contingency planning and reinforces the understanding that nontraditional movement, or even no movement, are valid options. Kaye (1982) has identified several options for growing within an organization: vertical movement, lateral movement, job enrichment (growing in place), realignment (moving down), and moving out (relocation).

Another way to help participants come to value a variety of options is to present charts depicting career path patterns. These have been identified by Michael Driver (1979) as linear, steady state, transitory, and spiral patterns (see Exhibit 2-11). In the workshop have participants identify the advantages and potential disadvantages of each of these patterns.

Information on career patterns and direction options is only the backdrop against which the real essence of information about work is presented. Preparing information about turnover by level or by major function within your organization, about staffing patterns, and about important feeder positions provides your career planners with very specific, important data to use.

Another important part in the career planning workshop deals with the specifics of work in different parts of the organization. Current organization charts, user-friendly job descriptions or profiles, and case studies presenting career moves leading to key target positions within the company are useful materials. Some companies prepare booklets describing work functions in different parts of the organization.

Having executives address the group on what it takes to succeed in various areas of the company and on available job opportunities in their areas can be extremely valuable. Executive visits could take the form of a panel discussion, or they might join the group for lunch one day, serving as resource people in informal discussions. You may even develop a video library with employees and executives from each functional area talking about their work. This approach allows your participants to gather information on as many areas as interest them.

If the group members are from a variety of different functions or locations, encourage them to serve as resources for one another so that they can learn about work in different parts of the company. They could do this in the class using information interviewing techniques, valuable skills for all career planners.

The world of work is changing so quickly that some career planning programs are now including activities and information that help participants to understand what work in the future is likely to entail. You can prepare this using planning information for your company, news reports on work trends, and special publications (e.g., *Occupational Outlook Handbook* or *Careers Tomor-*

Exhibit 2-12
Work in the Future

Mark each of these statements T (true) or F (false).

___ Experts predict that most people will work at home in the future.

___ The best jobs in all fields in the future will be technical.

___ By 1995, the United States will have improved manufacturing processes so that we are once again adding large numbers of people in our factories.

___ Telecommunications is no longer a growing career field.

___ The largest increase in jobs will be in service work.

___ Most service workers will make substantial incomes in the future.

___ In the future few people will work at one full-time job.

___ Entrepreneurship is a fad that seems to be diminishing.

---

row) presenting data on workplace trends. A sample exercise on work in the future is shown in Exhibit 2-12.

Whatever approach you take to present information about the world of work within your business, be sure that it is current, clear, and specific enough to add to what participants already know. It is also important that you allow sufficient opportunity for individual exploration and at the same time provide enough structure to guide the exploration. If you are using a career planning summary work sheet, include sections on this form to capture information about work.

❦ *Setting Life and Career Goals*

Even though a number of participants will have experience in setting goals, very few will have a systematic process for identifying goals for the various aspects of their lives and careers. Goal setting may seem simplistic to some, impossible to others. The key factor is to make sure that everyone recognizes how important goals are. Without them, we have no landmark for making day-to-day choices. Without goals, we are much more likely to hand over the responsibility for our careers to someone else, or to leave it to chance or fate.

Goals have an uncanny quality that mobilizes energies and resources so that things begin to happen once they are clearly articulated.

Primary techniques used for goal setting in career planning workshops include visioning and specifying goals for our lives. In imaging or visioning, participants create clear pictures of a point in their future. These pictures represent an ideal future, one in which everything that they hoped would happen has come to be. It is important that participants identify their work setting, how they spend their time, how they relate to other people at work, what kind of tools or technology are involved in their work, and what kind of things they experience as "successes" in their ideal futures.

To envision their career future, participants may develop a career collage, that is, a collection of pictures, photos, or drawings that represent different aspects of their future. Another method is guided imagery. In this technique, you need to create a quiet, relaxed setting. Then, after helping participants relax and prepare themselves to participate fully in the exercise, lead them through a journey into their future. With both of these techniques, it is especially important for participants to record the specific images or pictures that come to them as part of their ideal future.

A second primary technique used in goal setting is for everyone to specify at least one goal for several major areas of his or her life. Typically, participants are able to describe things they want to achieve in: family, health, finance, career, travel or leisure, skill development, and personal growth (spiritual, emotional development).

Regardless of the approach used, it is critical that the workshop provide an opportunity for participants to spell out these career goals. Making a written (and sometimes verbal) statement of goals, even if it will be revised considerably after more investigation, is an important step. "Fuzzy" goals are made stronger when they are stated them in terms that are specific, measurable, and time-bound.

The materials used in goal setting are often developed by the program designer. Sentence completions, exercises in which participants write news stories about their lives, and lists of areas for setting goals are often included. You may find that a videotape on goal setting adds variety and is a good learning aid for moving goals from an abstract concept to concrete reality.

If you are using a career planning summary worksheet, include a place for goal statements. Many programs encourage participants to establish both a long-range goal statement and a short-range statement. (An example of this might be "to become district manager of manufacturing operations by 1995; to become operations manager at my plant by 1992.") Other programs encourage participants to specify goals in terms of skills to be used, level of skill application, and broad descriptions of the work setting. (An example of this kind of goal is "to use my expertise in financial management and budgeting at a decision-making level to improve the financial operations of the Go-For-Broke Division.")

❦ *Making Career Decisions*

When career decision making is included in career planning workshops and seminars, it is usually an examination of different decision-making processes and ways to enhance participants' typical approach.

Approaches to making career decisions have been delineated in various ways. Janis and Wheeler (1978) describe four approaches: complacency, defensive avoidance, hypervigilance, and vigilance. Donald and Carlysle's (1985) eight styles for making life's choices are agonizing, compliant, delaying, fatalistic, impulsive, intuitive, paralytic, and rational. You may wish to have your participants jot down a few decisions they have made in recent months, large or small, and note the approach they used in making the choice. Important

Exhibit 2-13
Decision Matrix

Key Values and Weights	Decision Options		
Totals			

points to emphasize when discussing these activities are many different ways we make decisions; that how we make decisions about things that are largely inconsequential is not particularly important, but how we approach the major choices in life is important; and that some people fail to integrate rational (fact-based) approaches and intuitive (feeling-based) approaches. Most people have a basic approach to making decisions that works fairly well, and most people's decision styles can be improved by balancing natural tendencies.

Some career planning programs that use the *Myers-Briggs Type Indicator* in the individual assessment portion of the program find it extremely useful to describe how different MBTI types might approach life and career decisions. A decision matrix is often included as a tool for weighing alternatives and making choices. This allows participants to list and weigh subjective values and needs, as well as objective criteria, and to evaluate options based on these. Exhibit 2-13 is a sample decision matrix.

❦ *Reality Testing*

Reality testing is an important part of the career planning process, but also one that is very difficult to accomplish in a workshop or seminar unless there is a break in the program of several days or even a couple of weeks. In reality testing participants verify their personal perspectives regarding their skills, abilities, and options. Reality testing is done most often with other people whose opinions the career planner values—current managers, former supervisors, peers and colleagues, employees who report to them, personnel representatives, family members, and close friends. Reality testing may also require gathering more specific data about employment in certain occupations or departments.

If you are able to take a break in your program, structure the process for reality testing and have participants practice in class before they go off to do this by themselves. One exercise that may be useful is asking participants to prepare a brief statement of "how I see my career self" for reality testing with others in a small workshop group. Then have a series of questions (mostly open-ended questions) prepared to follow up the statement. This gives them experience in describing their career strengths and goals and practice in interviewing that can help them understand the perspectives of others.

If you cannot take a break in your program, do some in-class reality testing. Have participants look for consistencies and inconsistencies in the data they have collected about themselves and about work. Ask them to explore these with others in the group. Make yourself available to guide them through this process if they have difficulty. In addition, you will probably want to provide some structure for participants to do more reality testing when they leave the program.

The goal of reality testing is to reconcile data. Participants need to integrate what they can do, what they want to do, and what their options seem to be.

❦ *Action Planning*

The final phase of a career planning workshop or seminar is participants examining how to implement a plan for accomplishing their goals. The first phase is for participants to have a detailed, step-by-step sequence of actions needed to achieve their goals. This list evolves from a careful examination of goals and current career state. Steps in these action plans include such things as obtaining additional information, developing skills required for target positions, gaining appropriate experience, enrolling in formal education or other learning programs, and using resources inside and outside the company that can help them. These steps are usually listed with time frames for accomplishing them. The second part of action planning is to develop some specific skills in self-marketing: interviewing, résumé writing, using the company's job posting system, developing a career network, and finding support systems through professional organizations or community groups, as appropriate.

As employees are encouraged more and more to consider growing in the current job rather than moving to another position, the emphasis in action planning has shifted from gaining job search skills (such as résumé writing or interviewing) to gaining skills for negotiating to have more career needs met in the present position. This shift has caused preparing for a career discussion with managers to be moved to a place of importance in some career planning workshops and seminars. The steps and skills for participating in a career discussion are presented, and, often, discussions are rehearsed in role playing or on videotape. The best career discussions occur when both the manager and employee have planned carefully for the discussion and have been prepared by learning a simple sequence of steps to follow, and by learning the necessary communications skills. Career discussion is described in detail in Chapter 3.

The final step is to close the program in ways that increase the commitment of participants to follow through on the action plans they have developed. Sharing parts of these plans with the workshop group is one strategy for increasing commitment. Another is for participants to make a "contract" with the instructor (and perhaps another participant as well). This contract is for some action that the participant will take within a specified period of time, usually not more than two to four weeks out. The participant is then contacted in a few weeks to see what progress has been made and what additional help may be needed.

Close the program with encouragement and energy. The group will have worked hard. They need to leave with the feeling that the time in the program is an investment well worth making and that their most important work lies ahead.

Exhibit 2-14
Sample Evaluation

Career Management Skills Workshop
Feedback

Please let us know your reaction to this program. You do not need to sign this page, but we do ask that you complete it fully and honestly.

Part 1	**Agree**				**Disagree**
How much do you agree with the following statements?	⑤	④	③	②	①
1. I now have an action plan for managing my career.	⑤	④	③	②	①
2. I have specific information on my skills, interests, and values to use in ongoing career management.	⑤	④	③	②	①
3. I have information on how to find out about work and job options inside and outside the company.	⑤	④	③	②	①
4. The instructor for this course was knowledgeable about the subject and able to present it effectively.	⑤	④	③	②	①
Part 2	**High**				**Low**
5. How would you rate your skills in managing your career before coming to this workshop?	⑤	④	③	②	①
6. How would you rate your skills in managing your career now?	⑤	④	③	②	①

Part 3

We would also like to know your specific comments. (Use back if you need more room.)

7 What was the most useful part of the workshop for you?

8. What part of the workshop was least useful for you?

9. Are there parts of the workshop that you would like to see expanded? If so, what?

10. Would you recommend this program to other managers? Why or why not?

EVALUATION TECHNIQUES

Evaluation is never a simple matter. To evaluate a workshop or seminar adequately, your criteria for success must be clearly defined. For example, if success for your program is having classes filled (i.e., numbers of people attending), then registration data could be your evaluation. If success means more people in the organization making lateral moves or developing new skills to be more effective on their current jobs, then placement information or training enrollments might be important in your evaluation. If goals of your program include increased job satisfaction or reports that the company cares about the careers of its employees, then an attitude survey (or a portion of one) could play an important role in your evaluation. If you designed the workshop to develop specific skills (e.g., writing internal résumés) then a post-workshop sample of résumés, compared with a sample of résumés prepared by employees before they attended the program could supply the data you need. At a minimum, get reactions from participants using a form such as the one shown in Exhibit 2-14.

FOR FURTHER STUDY

Help in developing successful career planning workshops and seminars is available from a number of sources, such as the University of Michigan, American Management Association, and numerous small consulting companies. Annually, the American Society for Training and Development offers a series of career development–related workshops at its national conference. Other professional associations—the Society for Human Resource Management and the Human Resource Planning Society are two—offer programming in career development topics as well. Classic studies and recent titles that are useful include the following:

Bolles, Richard N. *What Color Is Your Parachute?* La Jolla, Calif.: Ten Speed Press, 1988.

Gutteridge, Thomas G., and Fred L. Otte. *Organizational Career Development: State of the Practice*. Alexandria, Va: American Society for Training and Development Press, 1983.

Hall, Douglas T., *Career Development in Organizations*. San Francisco, Calif.: Jossey-Bass, 1986.

Kaye, Beverly L., *Up Is Not the Only Way*. Englewood Cliffs, N.J.: Prentice Hall, 1982.

Leibowitz, Zandy, Caela Farren, and Beverly Kaye, *Designing Career Development Systems*. San Francisco: Jossey-Bass, 1986.

Schein, Edgar, *Career Dynamics*. Reading, Mass.: Addison-Wesley, 1978.

In addition, there are films and videotapes specifically on career planning, setting goals, and taking responsibility for your life.

For those who wish to develop a higher level of expertise in the career development field, courses of study are available through business schools, schools of education, and counseling departments in colleges and universities. If you want to know more about designing training, one good place to start is with Dugan Laird's *Approaches to Training and Development* (Reading, Mass.: Addison-Wesley, 1984).

CHAPTER 3

❦ ❦

The Manager's Role in Career Development

"I thought that developing people was the Training Department's responsibility," began Chris, a line manager. "Sure, as a manager, it's my job to make certain that my people grow in their performance on the job. I can't develop them for other jobs, though. I don't even know about many other jobs in this company."

"You're right, to a certain extent," responded Jim, the chair of the Career Development Task Force. "In fact, you are probably 100 percent correct for how things have been in the past. Now, though, we are recognizing that development is a shared responsibility. Certainly the organization has some responsibilities, including the provision of training and development for employees, but you have some responsibilities, too. You are not responsible for your employees' career development, but we do believe that you have some responsibilities for supporting and facilitating such development. That's why we are here to explore the manager's role in career development."

❦ *Value*

Every organization that wants to implement a system for helping employees manage their careers must at some point in the design of its career programs deal with the role of the manager in employee career development. For a successful career development program, you need your managers' buy-in and support.

Managers are powerful players in the career development process, often without realizing it. Some managers put forth a good deal of time and energy to develop their employees. All managers interact with employees about performance issues—the first step in any development process.

Few organizations have support staffs with sufficient time and resources to work with every employee individually. Managers, on the other hand, have ongoing interactions with their staff. Their day-to-day activities lead naturally into discussions about careers. Managers, therefore, need to understand how they can increase the value of other career-related programs.

Working with managers to define clearly their career development roles and then providing them with the tools and support to be effective in those roles help to ensure that career development will become an integral part of the organization's approach to human resource management.

This chapter discusses options for involving managers in employee career development and some programs to help managers learn basic skills for carrying out their roles.

❦ *Chapter Organization*

In this chapter you will find

1. Definitions of terms used in the discussion of the manager's role in career development
2. An overview of the roles typically belonging to managers
3. How the manager's role typically fits within the larger career development system
4. Important decisions you must make in regard to the manager's role
5. Techniques to prepare managers for their role
6. Sample materials used in preparing managers to be career development partners
7. Evaluation techniques to track the effectiveness of managers' participation in employee career discussions
8. Evaluation techniques to track the effects of programs to prepare managers for their roles
9. Resources for additional information

❦ *Learning Objectives*

In this chapter you will learn the questions and issues to be considered in developing appropriate roles for managers in a career development system. You will also learn about the techniques and materials used to provide the background and learning needed by managers to carry out their most common role, a participant in an employee career discussion. After reading this chapter you will be able to

1. Discuss the major roles that managers play in career development programs.
2. Describe the options for managers and some benefits and risks for each.
3. Begin to develop materials to help managers be successful in their employee career development roles.
4. Establish a plan for evaluating the effectiveness of managers in their roles and the effectiveness of programs to prepare them for these roles.
5. Find resources to help if you need more information.

DEFINITIONS

In this chapter you will find a couple of terms that have not been defined. *Manager's role* refers to the responsibilities and activities expected to be fulfilled by managers in organizational career development. These roles are defined differently by different organizations. In this chapter the most frequently found roles are described.

A *career discussion* is a planned discussion between a manager and an employee who are attempting jointly to clarify developmental options in the employee's current job, examine career issues in light of current job performance and goals of the organization, and/or clarify future career options for that employee (Otte and Hutcheson 1985). Participating in a career discussion with employees is one of the most common, and most effective, roles for managers.

OVERVIEW

The roles of managers in employee career development vary greatly, based on the organization's expectations and philosophy, the type and number of other resources that support employee development, and the skills and style of the manager.

One of the pioneers of organizational career development, Walter Storey describes the role of managers as "helping people with career planning by developing a climate that encourages committed, productive, effective people"(1976, vi). Helping managers learn to create this kind of climate, according to Storey, requires understanding of some rules for dealing with employee career development, the agenda that employees bring to you, and the agenda that you may take to employees. He emphasizes the career discussion interview as a vehicle for supporting employee career development.

The roles a manager may take could be depicted on a continuum, ranging from "not interfering" to "supporting and facilitating" career development for employees (see Exhibit 3-1). The minimum expected of a manager may be to "get out of the way," so that employee career development can happen. This manager *permits* career development to occur. The other end of the continuum exists when a manager is well versed in the options for employees, has excellent skills in discussions of career issues and options with employees, and believes that it is the role of a manager to promote the career development of employees in every way possible. This manager *supports and facilitates* career development.

In their research on the roles of managers, Leibowitz and Schlossberg (1981) identified nine ways that managers participate in the career development of their employees: communicator, counselor, appraiser, coach, mentor, adviser, broker, referral agent, and advocate. In examining roles for managers, other researchers tend to emphasize one or the other of these nine roles. For example, Meckel (1981) has focused on the role of counselor and Jones, Kaye, and Taylor (1981) have emphasized career coach.

Organizations now tend to define appropriate roles for their managers and to include some preparation for managers, usually information and training on their role in the career process. These programs provide a forum for discussion on the issues related to managers' participation. They typically provide information about the organization's career system and resources for understanding work in the organization, and they offer managers training in coaching and in conducting career discussions.

Exhibit 3-1
Continuum of Appropriate Roles for Managers' Involvement in Employee Career Development

◄────────────────────────►

Not interfering	Supporting and facilitating

THE MANAGER'S ROLE IN THE LARGER CAREER DEVELOPMENT SYSTEM

Most career development systems emphasize that the employee is ultimately responsible for his or her own career. Most also emphasize the critical role of managers in helping employees accept this responsibility and effectively manage their own careers. Even in those organizations with few specific career-related roles outlined for managers, descriptions of the career processes often emphasize how important it is for managers to use career development as a central focus for managing performance.

In some career systems, the manager-employee career discussion is seen as the focal point of all the career programs. It is this discussion that takes the information from career planning workshops or workbooks, focuses it on the realities of the business and the employee's performance and capabilities, and results in a development plan that has the manager's support for implementation (see Exhibit 3-2).

Career discussions with employees may lead to the use of other career-related processes and programs. For example, managers may refer employees who need more information to the career center, or they may ask an employee who seems to lack focus to visit a career adviser or counselor. The career discussion may also identify additional training, education, or special assignments needed to help the employee accomplish agreed-upon career goals.

DECISIONS TO MAKE IN DESIGNING THE MANAGER'S ROLE

Early in the process of installing an employee career development program, questions will arise about the role of managers in relation to the total set of career services. Before you decide that career discussions with employees are to be conducted by managers, the following questions need to be addressed.

What is the most appropriate role for managers in this organization in relation to employee career development? An answer for this question requires that you give serious consideration to several related issues: what you would really like managers to be able to do to support the other parts of your career development system, the skills that your managers currently have, the career issues that the managers themselves are facing, and the support you have from various levels of management. This information will not define the role your managers should play, but it will give you insight into what roles they may easily take on and what roles will require more coaching, education, and training.

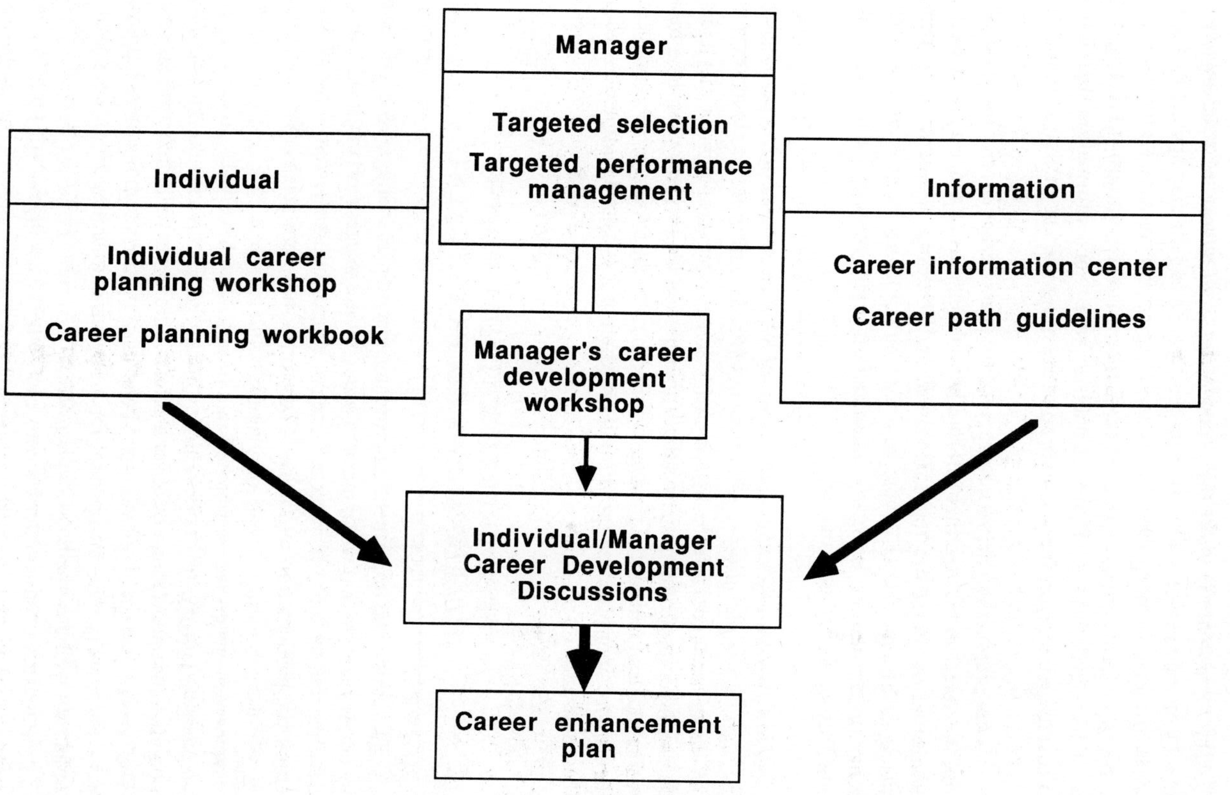
Manager
Targeted selection
Targeted performance management
Individual
Individual career planning workshop
Career planning workbook
Information
Career information center
Career path guidelines
Manager's career development workshop
Individual/Manager Career Development Discussions
Career enhancement plan

Who will actually make the decisions on what managers' roles will be? Ideally, no one person will make this decision. Data gathering and discussions can help managers recognize what the most appropriate roles are for themselves. Using input from managers, or even a task force made up primarily of managers, can aid you in defining their roles in realistic ways. Such information also helps to ensure their support for whatever roles are designated as theirs.

What preparation do managers need for their career development roles? You may elect to put together informative publications or videotapes, a guide or manual outlining the responsibilities, and/or design a workshop to help managers become career developers. For most managers, new attitudes and behaviors are needed, so many organizations prefer training backed up with other resources and information.

How can managers be made aware of what employees are experiencing through career planning seminars or workbooks, and how employee expectations of managers will be influenced? Some organizations brief managers on employee programs; others supply information about these programs in a workshop designed for the manager. Still others require managers to complete their own career planning program in preparation for assisting employees with their careers.

TECHNIQUES USED IN DEVELOPING THE MANAGER'S ROLE COMPONENT

Designing and implementing programs that prepare managers for their role in employee career development is vital for the success of the total career development system. If managers are not supporting the system, obstacles to employee participation will arise. Sometimes these obstacles are subtle, such as simply not taking action or making comments like "we'll get to career development when we've finished this project...we have work to do." Even when managers say they believe in developing people, if they do not find time or budget to support their employees' efforts, employees will likely lose interest. The risks may seem to outweigh the benefits of participation for these employees. Thus, every other component for the program may be underutilized if this one is not well designed and implemented.

Managers need to interact with each other, as well as with other people involved in the development and operation of the career system, to ensure that their assumptions and beliefs about the career programs are in line with the attitudes needed to be effective in their roles. Furthermore, the skills required for discussing career issues with employees are interactive. Therefore, programs on the manager's role are most commonly presented in a workshop format. Exhibit 3-3 shows a sample agenda for a one-day workshop on the role of the manager.

The following discussion will guide you in selecting content appropriate for your program, and the sections on variations will help you see what other methods you might use to accomplish similar results.

Exhibit 3-3
Sample Agenda for a One-Day Workshop on the Manager's Role

Welcome and introductions

Program overview

Define manager's role in developing employees

Define career discussions

Benefits and risks

Overview of process

Introduce skills

- Setting the stage
- Listening
- Responding
- Developing alternatives
- Reaching joint conclusions

Model of career discussion 1

Model of career discussion 2 and tough issues

Rehearsal 1

Rehearsal 2

New Roles in organizations

Organizational values and career discussions

Action planning, evaluation, and conclusion
Resources

❦ *Integrating the Manager's Role with Other Human Resource Management Processes*

This introductory segment of the program is designed to give managers the big picture of career development within the organization.

Needs met: Managers need to see where their career development efforts fit in relation to other program components. They are more confident to move ahead and learn about their role and how to implement it when they know what else will be happening and how these other components support each other. Managers typically require some encouragement to add any new responsibilities to their already full schedules. This early part of the workshop demonstrates how career development can integrate other human resource management and development activities that managers already perform (performance appraisals, development planning, succession planning) into a more meaningful overall process.

Results desired: A successful beginning of the manager's role program will be evidenced by

1. The manager's willingness to move on and explore his or her role in career development.
2. Agreement that the manager does, by the nature of his or her management job, have a stake in employee career development.
3. Recognition of how the manager's career development activities fit with other human resource management and development activities in the company.

At this point, it is good if managers show enthusiasm for employee career development and their role(s) in it. This is not necessary, however. Managers are more likely to express enthusiasm after they have examined the benefits and risks involved, heard more exactly what is expected of them, and worked on skills to increase their effectiveness.

Information and exercises typically included: To begin the manager's role program, you will probably want to include a warm-up exercise to help managers begin thinking about how they do (or can) help employees with their careers. Exhibit 3-4 is an example of one exercise managers can do and report on as they introduce themselves to the group. This kind of exercise sets a participative tone for the day and moves quickly to the content you want to cover. Other information typically included in this introductory segment is a statement (in person, on tape, or on paper) from the CEO or other executive officer pointing

Exhibit 3-4
Introductory Exercise for a Program on the Manager's Role

How Others Help In Your Development

Most of us at some time in our careers have benefited by the advice, support, or coaching of some other person. Think back to a time when someone helped you to grow or develop in your career. Select one example that you consider especially useful and describe it below.

Now, as you listen to others describe how they have been helped in their careers, list below the many different ways in which this kind of influence can occur.

out the perceived value for developing employee careers and encouraging managers to take full advantage of the information to be presented.

These activities help managers feel more comfortable about senior management's support and provide the security of knowing that there are other sources of information and guidance to supplement their individual roles.

Variations: If you are not introducing managers to their career development roles with a meeting or workshop, you may develop an informative videotape. Another option is a publication (pamphlet or bulletin) outlining the career development programs and how they fit with other ongoing human resource management and development programs. Placing these materials in a career center will encourage managers to visit the center and learn more about supports for their role as they are being introduced to materials developed specifically for them.

Another desirable option, if you have several individuals involved in developing and implementing career system components, is to ask those people to explain their areas of responsibility. These presentations allow the key players in the program to be more visible to the managers and encourage direct interaction to answer questions or address issues.

❦ *Examining Benefits and Risks*

A topic that needs to be addressed early on is the perceived benefits and risks of developing employees, or more specifically, of having a program to promote the role of managers in employee career development.

Needs met: An exercise or discussion on the benefits and risks for developing employees helps managers express their hopes and apprehensions for career development. It allows the facilitator or instructor to uncover and put to rest any myths that prevail about what career programs can or cannot accomplish. Managers may come to the program uncomfortable because they believe that the goal of career development is upward movement. If this is not readily available for employees, they fear raising employee expectations. Frank, open discussions that acknowledge real risks, as well as benefits, can help establish credibility for the program.

Results desired: When discussion about the benefits and risks for developing employees is successful, managers will have

1. Voiced their fears about such issues as limited movement within the company, time required to develop employees, unrealistic employee expectations, and the like
2. Acknowledged that helping to develop employees has very tangible benefits for the employee, for themselves as managers, and for the organization
3. Seen you (the facilitator) as a realist who wants them to know the potential pitfalls so that they can be avoided or managed.

Information and exercises typically included: In a workshop setting, managers can either react to prepared lists of benefits and risks or they can generate their own lists. Interviews with others in the company to identify benefits and risks frequently mentioned or considered most important can validate this exercise and help managers see that others share their feelings. Concluding the exercise calls for skill in helping managers draw some positive, yet realistic, conclusions.

Variations: If you are not presenting managers with information about their role in career development through workshops, you may wish to make printed information available to help them deal with their very real fears about the possible consequences of encouraging employee career development. If you have video capability, this topic lends itself nicely to a "people on the street" interview format. You may wish to interview several people at different levels in the organization to hear their perceptions about possible gains and losses.

❦ *Defining the Manager's Role*

Needs met: Managers want as clear and concise a description as possible of what they are being asked to do. This section provides the opportunity for them to explore their role and become comfortable with it.

Results desired: When this portion of the program is successful, managers will be able to tell you exactly how their role in employee career development is defined. They will also be able to describe what activities and responsibilities are included and what are not. Further they will be able to differentiate among their role, the role of the individual employee, and the role of the company.

Information and exercises typically included: The roles defined for managers within the organization dictate the information included here. Definitions, descriptions, or models may be presented, as appropriate. Exhibit 3-5 shows how the different roles have been described for one organization. Leibowitz et al. (1986) offer a model of four different roles for managers and the behaviors associated with each. These are presented in Exhibit 3-6.

Perhaps the simplest widely used description of the manager's role is that it supports and facilitates development while promoting a match of individual and organizational goals, similar to the approach offered by Otte and Hutcheson (1985). Although this description does not specify activities, it does clearly acknowledge that the responsibility for development is with the individual. The manager is responsible for enabling the individual to grow and develop within

Exhibit 3-5
Roles in Career Development

Individual

- Accept responsibility for your own career
- Assess your interests, skills, and values
- Seek out career information and resources
- Establlish goals and career plans
- Utilize development opportunities
- Talk with your manager about your career
- Follow through on realistic career plans

Manager

- Provide timely performance feedback
- Provide developmental assignments and support
- Participate in career development discussions
- Support employee development plans

Organization

- Communicate mission, policies, and procedures
- Provide training and development opportunities
- Provide career information and career programs
- Offer a variety of career options

the boundaries of meeting the needs of the individual and the business. This support can take different forms—coaching, on-the-job assignments, feedback, and the like.

Developing Skills for the Career Discussion

Regardless of the roles defined for managers in employee career development, the most common activity is the career discussion. This discussion provides the opportunity for following up on employee career planning efforts,

Exhibit 3-6
Four Roles for Managers in Employee Development

Coach	*Appraiser*	*Adviser*	*Referral Agent*
Listens Clarifies Probes Defines concerns	Gives feedback Clarifies standards Clarifies job responsibilities	Generates options Helps set goals Recommends/advises	Links employee to resources/people Consults on action plan

From Leibowitz, Z.B., Farren, C., and Kaye, B.L. *Designing Career Development Systems*. San Francisco: Jossey-Bass, 1986. p. 126 [Table 9].

giving feedback, coaching, collaborating on specific development plans, and addressing other matters identified by the employee or the manager.

Needs met: The career discussion is the primary vehicle for enabling managers to carry out their other career-related activities and roles. This discussion, most often initiated by the employee, is the opportunity for an open, honest dialogue between the manager and the employee about the employee's career and how it can grow and develop. Employees need to hear their managers' opinions and to solicit their support for development and/or career plans. Managers need the discussion so that they can express their perspectives, coach employees on their career plans, and become a career partner supporting employees' development.

One major benefit of productive, supportive career discussion is their tendency to generate better relationships between employees and managers. When each understands the other, new respect and commitment are likely to result.

Results desired: Successful career discussions have several important results:

1. Managers know their employees' work-related goals and interests.
2. Employees and managers agree on the employees' next steps for development.

3. Employees understand how their managers view their performance, development needs, and options.
4. Employees and managers share a clearer understanding about how the employees' needs can be met (or met in part) on the current job.
5. Resources for accomplishing the steps agreed-upon in the discussion are identified.

Information and exercises typically included: Preparing managers for career development discussions with their employees requires that new applications be made for some skills that managers may already possess. In some cases, these skills do not exist, or are not adequate, for effective career discussions. In the planning of the structure and content of your program, the skills of your managers need to be carefully weighed. Even though the skills are similar to those that managers use in other settings, their use in the career development discussion is a complex application.

❦ *Following Five Critical Steps*

This discussion addresses the critical steps necessary for successful career discussions and some skills managers need in order to move successfully through these steps. Exhibit 3-7 summarizes these for you.

Setting the Stage: The skills needed to accomplish this step call for managers to create the physical and psychological environments that make it easier for both the manager and the employee to feel comfortable discussing even potentially risky issues. The physical setting should be relaxed and private. A conference room or office (with seating away from the desk) works well. A positive psychological environment can be created by demonstrating the importance of the conference by establishing time and date well ahead of the discussion and by having both parties do some preparation work. At the time of the conference, the manager reinforces this positive climate by being positive and friendly.

Active listening: In the career discussion, active listening is especially important and the payoffs are numerous. Some of the major benefits are building the trust level, so that the conversation is more honest and open, increasing the likelihood that real issues, not just symptoms, will be dealt with, and creating an atmosphere of acceptance. This acceptance of shared viewpoints and differences is critical for moving ahead and establishing alternatives.

As managers use active listening skills in a career discussion, they may find it useful to focus on three goals:

Exhibit 3-7
Steps in the Career Discussion Process

Step	How to Accomplish	Outcome
Set the stage	Devote time to prepare.	Meeting is efficient, stress is reduced.
	Establish time and place.	Discussion occurs in appropriate environment without interruptions.
	Create a relaxed atmosphere.	Encourages trust and openness.
	Be positive and friendly.	Both feel comfortable.
	Share expectations.	Both know what to expect.
Listen	Hear concerns.	Nondefensive listening.
	Clarify issues.	Common understanding.
	Listen for themes.	Your perceptions are reality-tested.
	Look for assessment of skills.	Both agree on strengths and developmental areas.
Respond	Share your perceptions and insights.	You demonstrate trust. Employee knows your viewpoints.
	Be open and flexible.	You learn another viewpoint.
	Be specific, give examples.	Your employee understands your position.
	Reality Test.	Encourages realistic decisions for both you and employee.
Develop alternatives	Be creative.	Numerous ideas generated.
	Begin with current assignments.	Promotes moving ahead.
	Explore all types of development opportunities.	Growth not limited.
Reach joint conclusions	Summarize key discussion points.	Both know discussion outcome.
	Identify action steps.	Identifies next steps.
	Set a date for follow-up.	Ensures ongoing activity.

1. Hear concerns by listening "between the words."
2. Clarify issues—verify the concerns that you think you are hearing.
3. Listen for themes—issues that surface in a number of different ways in the discussion become themes that may be important to point out.

Responding: This is the point in the career discussion at which managers have the opportunity to share the viewpoints, perspectives, and information they feel are important to move the discussion ahead in realistic ways. Five frequently used responses in the career discussion are:

1. *Summarizing*—frequent summaries let the employee know the manager is listening and ensure that the conversation is on track.
2. *Sharing perceptions*—when managers are able to share how they see the employee (e.g., "I see you as a strong contributor") and gently challenge information the employee has presented (e.g., "Another way some might see what happened in the Big Time project is..."), the career discussion moves ahead in positive and productive paths.
3. *Confronting inconsistencies*—managers may need tactfully, even tentatively, to confront conflicting messages that the employee is sending.
4. *Providing information*—managers sometimes have specific information about company directions, future projects, or other things that affect the employee's development plans. The career discussion provides an opportune time to share whatever information can be shared.
5. *Reality testing*—Employees need to think through the probability of succeeding in their selected career directions. Managers can offer their perceptions of reality, and can encourage employees to check these out with others whose opinions they respect.

Developing alternatives: This skill requires abilities in creativity and problem solving and information about opportunities within the organization. Often managers take the easy way out and move directly to training programs as alternatives to helping the employee grow and develop. More meaningful options may emerge if this is kept as a last resort. Focus first on-the-job, special assignment, or individualized exploration.

Reaching joint conclusions: This is the "handshake" at the end of the career development discussion. Managers need to be able to summarize key points of the discussion, identify action steps, and review follow-up plans. It is important that managers not take responsibility for the next steps, but leave these to the employee.

Methods to help managers become skilled and comfortable in using these steps and skills generally require some practice exercises in each of the target skills. Managers often believe they are more skilled in an area than a skills practice will verify. So it is good for them to have opportunities to engage in activities, evaluate their effectiveness, and improve upon or "upgrade" the skills.

Since this part of the program is attempting to establish effective behaviors for your managers to use, it is wise to offer behavioral models. A videotape or role playing (scripted and rehearsed) can provide valuable insights for your managers on how to handle different parts of the career discussion. Then they need to practice the skills they have been learning. Skills practice is often eliminated from manager's role training programs to save time, but the cost is significant. The effectiveness of all the rest of the learning may be lost.

❦ *Following Up on the Career Discussion*

It would be difficult to overstate the importance of following up with your managers and with employees on their career discussions. Slavenski and Buckner (1988) point out that following up to ensure that the planned development is actually taking place is one of the soundest innovations in career development in recent years. Without action, career discussions will lose their momentum, as they should. Follow-up emphasizes that these discussions are to be realistic and productive.

❦ *Variations*

Without a workshop format, it is difficult to change managers' behaviors and develop the skills needed for a productive career discussion. Here are some options to consider when bringing your managers together is difficult or impossible:

1. Develop an interactive video learning program. Although expensive, this is the next best option to bringing your managers together in groups. Since consistency is ensured in the delivery, it may even have some advantages not possible to attain in "live" delivery of the material.
2. Put together a list of resources to help managers develop skills on their own (ongoing training programs within the company, community-based training, readings, etc.).
3. Organize a question/answer problem-solving network. If your managers are linked through personal computers, this might be a great way to do problem solving on how to handle potentially difficult situations in career discussions. You could accomplish part of this by producing print materials, audiotapes, or brief videos to support your managers in their career discussion efforts.

MATERIALS AND RESOURCES NEEDED

Developing a program to help managers participate fully and appropriately in employee career development requires examining or developing a number of resources.

1. The organization's mission, goal statements, and company philosophy on developing people help you get started on defining the role for your managers.
2. Program materials will need to be developed (or purchased). Participant's materials, learning exercises, and media to support your program must be obtained or developed. Some published materials that may be useful for your design include

   - *Career Dimensions III* (Storey 1976). A how-to-do-it guide for the manager to use in coaching employees about their career and for dealing with tough questions and messages.
   - *Organizational Career Development: State of the Practice* (Gutteridge and Otte 1985). A description of practices in organizations reputed to have effective career development programs.

3. Commercially available programs to train managers in their role may fit your needs. Check with professional associations, with human resource associations, or with consulting organizations.

EVALUATION TECHNIQUES

To evaluate the effectiveness of the manager's role component, you will need to gather information on

1. The reaction of managers to the training and information made available to them. This can be done with a checklist, survey, or interview soon after they have attended a program or received information.

2. The degree to which the information is being used to improve the overall effectiveness of your career development program. Are career discussions taking place? If so, what is the result of these discussions? Are discussions leading to development plans being implemented? You may wish to audit (in person or with audiotapes) some career discussions to determine what is working well and what may need to be improved. Since this may be threatening or awkward, you may accomplish much of the same results by interviewing selected managers and employees about the career discussion. Prepare a list of questions, so you will obtain similar information from a number of people.

From this you may find specific concerns or difficulties that can be addressed. Improving the quality of discussions may involve coaching the manager, coaching the employee, and/or shifting the emphasis for part of the training, with support materials to deal with the difficulties.

For Further Study

The manager's role in career development and, specifically, the career discussion are topics included in a number of books and references in the area of human resource development. Of particular interest for this topic, in addition to those described in the materials section, are the following:

Hanson, Marlys, "Implementing a Career Development Program," *Training and Development Journal,* 35, 7 (July 1981), 80–90.

Jones, Pamela R., Beverly Kaye, and Hugh R. Taylor, "You Want Me to Do What?" *Training and Development Journal,* 35, 7 (July 1981), 56–62.

Kaye, Beverly, *Up Is Not the Only Way.* Englewood Cliffs, N.J.: Prentice Hall, 1982.

Leibowitz, Zandy, Caela Farren, and Beverly Kaye, *Designing Career Development Systems.* San Francisco: Jossey-Bass, 1986.

Leibowitz, Zandy, and Nancy Schlossberg, "Training Managers for Their Role in a Career Development System" *Training and Development Journal,* 35, 7 (July 1981). 72–79.

Merman, Stephen, and Zandy Leibowitz, eds., *Career Development Systems: Questions Worth Asking and Answers Worth Questioning.* Alexandria, Va.: American Society for Training and Development, 1987.

CHAPTER 4

❦ ❦

Managing the Career Counseling Component

Susan is a young professional who attended the pilot career planning seminar sponsored by the Career Development Task Force. She developed a career plan in the seminar. Now, however, Susan is apprehensive about presenting the plan to her supervisor, vaguely fearing negative reactions. She visits the career counselor whose services she heard about in the seminar. The career counselor assists her in bringing the fears to the surface, anticipating various scenarios, and practicing how to make the presentation. Susan feels that there is still some chance that it might not work well. Having the counselor as a back up helps her to have the courage to face the manager, however. The result most likely will be a career discussion that leads to joint decisions benefiting both Susan and the organization. If her supervisor reacts negatively, though, Susan can go back to the counselor and plan what to do next.

VALUE

This scenario points out the sophisticated skills needed in career counseling. Other career development practices described in this book can be learned relatively easily through reading, observation, and experimenting with pilot projects. By contrast, career counseling requires a trained professional. Typically, this person has at least a master's degree in counseling or equivalent training, perhaps in social work, plus supervised practice in career counseling.

This chapter is important to anyone implementing an employee career development system, for several reasons. When most people hear the term *career development*, they think of career counseling, but they are not clear as to what it is or what it can provide. They have little idea what a career counselor actually does and do not understand the various types of counseling. The discussion in this chapter will assist managers, career development specialists, and other human resource professionals to determine if their organization needs to add or to revise a career counseling component. It will give you the background you need for making decisions, including staffing decisions, and will prepare you to talk with career counselors about your needs.

❦ *Chapter Organization*

In this chapter you will find

1. Definitions of terms used in describing career counseling
2. An overview of career counseling
3. An explanation of the place of career counseling in the larger career development system
4. Decisions you need to make about adding career counseling and a brief discussion of each one
5. An overview of three approaches to career counseling
6. Some thoughts on situations requiring other approaches
7. Recommended evaluation techniques, with examples of forms
8. Resources for further study

❦ *Learning Objectives*

After reading this chapter you will be able to

1. Explain to decision makers what career counseling is, how it fits into a career development system, and how it can meet organizational needs
2. Outline the decisions to be made regarding the addition or revision of a career counseling component and clarify the issues involved
3. Specify criteria to be considered when hiring a career counselor
4. Describe how a career counseling program could be evaluated
5. Plan further study as you need it

DEFINITIONS

The term *career counseling* refers to a function performed by professionals trained in counseling who specialize in working with employees seeking personalized assistance in resolving career concerns. The most common concern is career indecision or indecisiveness, which may involve lack of career information, lack of skill in gaining such information, unwillingness to decide (even when the needed information is known), motivational conflicts, or a combination of these factors. When indecisiveness is present, or when there are motivational conflicts that create difficulty in decision making, counseling is required. By contrast, if the problem is merely lack of information or information-seeking skill, career advising (as described in Chapter 5) may be sufficient.

Some employees have difficulties in relating to people with whom they work, and the interpersonal problems interfere with their careers. Significant behavioral changes may be required that can be accomplished only with the help of a skilled counselor because such changes usually depend on significantly increased self-awareness. Other employees have difficulties in implementing career plans; their good intentions do not lead to appropriate actions. Again, self-management skills must be learned, and these too, depend on gaining self-awareness.

Professional counselors can also administer and interpret individual assessment instruments or psychological tests to assist employees in developing better self understanding as a basis for decision making.

For all types of problems the counseling relationship itself is a key ingredient in the process. This relationship is one of high trust, openness to expressing feelings, and intimacy similar to that established in *personal counseling*, which addresses psychological problems of a developmental nature, and in *therapy*, which seeks to restore the ability of more psychologically disturbed individuals to function well. Professional skills are needed to create and manage this type of relationship. However, the other career counseling techniques described below also require professional training to ensure appropriate use.

Career counseling usually requires more time than career advising; it takes less time than personal counseling or therapy. However, career problems rarely exist in isolation from other concerns, and there is a great deal of overlap among forms of counseling and therapy. Practitioners have difficulty defining and distinguishing among them, as has been documented by Gutteridge and Otte (1983). General differences, as discussed above, are summarized in Exhibit 4-1.

Exhibit 4-1
Career Counseling Compared with Some One-On-One Practices*

Dimensions	Career Advising	Career Counseling	Personal Counseling	Therapy
Problem focus	Rational clarification of career plans and available resources, both personal and organizational	More thorough self-assessment and exploration of emotional or skill difficulties affecting career progress	Overcoming emotional barriers to personal growth and relationships	Overcoming more dysfunctional behavior
Time involved	Up to 3 sessions of 30 to 60 minutes	From 1 to 10 sessions of up to 60 minutes	An hour weekly for up to several months	May be several hours weekly for years
Feelings expressed	Weak/strong	Deep	Deep	Deep
Trust required	Moderate	High	High	High
Training required+	One day	2 to 5 years	2 to 5 years	2 to 5 years

*Distinctions are not as clear-cut as they appear.

+One-day training for advising assumes good, basic interpersonal skills. The 2 to 5 years suggested for the other practices are a broad range because some therapists and counselors work under supervision of more highly trained specialists. They have less training.

OVERVIEW

Career counseling can take many forms, depending on the needs of employees, the approaches to career counseling used by the counselor, and the reasons for implementing the practice. In this chapter we discuss some approaches or models in some detail and the employee needs that they meet. See Crites (1981) for a summary of the various career counseling approaches.

All forms of career counseling have one major thing in common. Either individual or group sessions are led by a trained professional whose objective is to draw out and help employees to resolve their career concerns. Fairly serious emotional issues are involved. No preplanned agenda is essential, because the individual concerns upon which the counselor focuses are brought to the surface during the sessions. It may take several hours to define an employee's problem, although that one step is a major accomplishment. As in many situations, defining the problem may be 95 percent of the solution.

Typically, at the beginning, employees are not able to articulate fully their problems. If they could do so, counselors would not be needed unless the employees required assistance in locating resources. They could just begin seeking help in resolving their difficulties.

Employee problems that can be addressed through career counseling, and that are difficult to handle through other career development practices, vary greatly. The problems are as varied as (1) not understanding difficulties in working with a supervisor, peers, or subordinates; (2) being unsure of why they feel stuck in their current position; (3) being unwilling to accept estimates, made by others, of their skills, abilities, interests, or aptitudes; (4) experiencing difficulties in making a career decision; and (5) balancing career and other aspects of their lives. In each case emotional blind spots are involved. Employees need to develop more self-awareness and to resolve value conflicts. These needs generally are not met through common sense discussions with a manager or with friends.

Each problem reflects an unmet need. Attending to these needs benefits both the organization and the individual. The organization benefits from the employee's greater commitment to work tasks; for the employee, work is more satisfying.

CAREER COUNSELING IN THE LARGER CAREER DEVELOPMENT SYSTEM

Career counseling increases the efficiency of the other components in a career development system. In turn, the other components provide resources to employees that allow counselors to concentrate on what they uniquely can provide: help in cutting through emotional barriers or behavioral deficits that impede effective functioning.

Other components typically work well with about one third of the employees using them, provide satisfactory service for another one third to one half, but do not work as well for the rest. Most likely both the employees and the staff offering other career services are baffled. They are unclear as to why the desired outcomes are not reached. Blaming doesn't resolve the difficulty. Unearthing the cause through counseling may lead to redirecting efforts and success in solving the problem.

For example, Steve may go through a career planning seminar and emerge with a career plan based on assessed interests and values. He then shares this plan with his manager during a career discussion, and joint decisions are made. Steve is to enroll in a college course to develop new skills that can be used in the current job and that will help him to qualify for a promotion. The manager is to allow flexible scheduling of work time to permit Steve to take the class during the day.

Steve does not, however, complete the paperwork to get enrolled. When the manager inquires how plans for school are progressing, Steve makes excuses and promises to finish the paperwork. Steve wonders to himself what is wrong and what is to be done. Telling the manager that he has decided not to go to school is unsatisfactory; it may look like a lack of interest that could damage his chances for a promotion. Steve remembers that the career counselor, Dr. Phillips, visited the career seminar and explained that getting stuck in this way is common. Dr. Phillips had suggested that any employee who experiences this drop by for a chat; so, while on lunch break, Steve goes by her office. Dr. Phillips is with someone else, and Steve makes an appointment for the next day.

The next day, Dr. Phillips asks Steve to explain briefly what caused him to come for a visit. After about 15 minutes of discussion, it seems clear that Steve anticipates that the paperwork for college admission could take as much as four or five hours; he hates that type of paperwork and dreads starting the project. Together they talk about approaches to the problem, then agree that Steve will (1) work one hour after dinner each night, starting that night, after explaining the plan to his wife, (2) leave a phone message each day for Dr. Phillips reporting that the hour was put in, (3) work until the paperwork is completed, and (4) celebrate success and give himself a reward by taking his wife to dinner at a place they both like a great deal but where they seldom go because it is a bit expensive. A week later, Steve leaves a message that the paperwork is done and that the dinner was great.

This case is simple, common, and one that lends itself readily to the application of simple self-management behavior modification techniques. Yet many people never learn to break dreaded self-development tasks into small, manageable pieces, to plan a schedule, and to plan a celebration of, and reward for, success. Several things made it possible for Steve: (1) He had a career plan he wanted to implement. (2) The counselor was there. (3) The counselor was known through her visit to the seminar and was perceived as a "safe" person with whom to talk. (4) The counselor had indicated that the problem was a common one, taking away some of the fear typically involved in visiting a counselor of any type and raising hope for a solution.

Steve needed to learn a simple self-management skill, but he was unaware of it. No emotional difficulties were involved; the problem was a simple one. However, the counselor's half hour with Steve made it possible for the time spent in the career planning seminar to pay off. It also opened the way for Steve to invest time off the job in further education that would benefit both him and his work unit. The career planning seminar, the supervisory career discussion, and the finances available through the tuition reimbursement program allowed Dr. Phillips to concentrate on what only she could add to make the total system work. Without the counselor component, an evaluation of the career planning seminar and the career discussion would have suggested that they were not working, and the tuition reimbursement program would not have been used. The cause of the failure of the other components probably would not have been known.

Highly trained career counselors can help people learn to manage their careers and their behavior. This moves employees toward being more valuable resources for the organization. It makes other components work better.

Still, in some situations it may be appropriate to use counselors with lower levels of training.

Assume that one counselor with a master's degree is hired to supervise career advisers housed in career centers at a number of different locations. Furthermore, initially these centers are the major career development system thrust, without career planning workshops or supervisory career discussions. The role of the counselor is different in this case. The major task is selecting and training career advisers drawn from within the organization. The counselor may also interpret tests taken by employees who come to a center seeking a sense of direction when they are unsure which career options to explore. An adviser is trained to administer the tests; the counselor helps the employee to understand the results. The counselor is needed at this point to ensure that all relevant issues are raised and that the results are interpreted correctly.

Decisions to Make in Designing the Career Counseling Component

When considering whether to institute career counseling, an organization should answer several questions and make a number of decisions in order to have the most effective career counseling program. Questions include the following, and answering one of them usually has implications for answering the others:

Why add career counseling? Is it needed? This question brings up organizational culture issues. Basic attitudes toward employees and toward counseling will be uncovered. Some people feel that "real men" or "real managers" or "real professionals" don't need counseling; they can handle their own problems. They feel that employees ought to be able to understand themselves; seeking the help of a counselor is a sign of weakness. These attitudes can color the answers to the other questions. So discuss this question. You need a "buy-in" for the ideas that it is OK to seek career counseling and that the organization can benefit. Benefits from this component are similar to those of the other components: better alignment of individual and organizational goals, the individual commitment that accompanies alignment, and the related organizational improvements.

What type of career counselor do we want? What hiring criteria do we use? Common approaches to career counseling are briefly described below. The counselor may prefer one approach to the others or may use pieces of each approach, depending on client needs. You need to ask if this is of concern to the organization. There will also be differences according to level of training. A person with a doctorate degree will be able to deal with deeper, more personal concerns than can a person with a master's degree, but the costs will be more. A broader range of skills, perhaps even an understanding of organizational development and the possibility of being an in-house trainer for human resources staff, may also come with the doctorate, if the prospective hire has been preparing to work in a business setting. Also the "fit" of the personality of this person with other human resource personnel is critical if all the career development components are to support one another well.

Credibility with management is an issue, as is the amount of experience in other types of work roles. Consider what the person needs to know about the work you do and what attitudes toward this organization are needed in order to function within this culture. One cultural issue is whether you want a career counselor who waits for employees to make contact or one who takes the initiative in talking with them. The type of service provided and the impact on the organization will be different with initiators in contrast to sustainers. Finally, you may decide to use outside counselors in private practice for referrals, much like an employee assistance program uses outside treatment facilities. One consideration here is that insurance is unlikely to cover the costs, and cost containment may be an issue.

Where will the counselor be located? How will services be made available elsewhere? These issues need to be considered in close connection with the next two below. The type of duties assigned, where these services are needed, and to whom the person reports will affect the location chosen. The location should be accessible to employees and be in a place they are willing to visit. Having a central office and remote sites that are periodically visited may be needed. Covering a territory of several states may be possible, if there is a feasible number of employees involved and if the counseling approach allows for telephone work. Much can be done by phone, but the counselor will need to be active in initiating contact with scattered employees, not waiting for them to call.

To whom will the counselor report? Superficially the answer is obvious: Career counselors are part of human resource development; therefore, they should report to the head of HRD. However, one organization known to us had both the career counselor and the employee assistance coordinator sharing a suite and reporting directly to the chairman of the board. The idea was to protect their professional positions, to ensure that there was no pressure to perform unrelated duties, to allow them to make easy referrals to one another, and to emphasize the importance of the services. You need to ask what perception of the component is created by where it is placed in the organizational structure.

Are other responsibilities to be assigned? The counselor could have management and/or training responsibilities. Natural additional duties include supervising other career counselors or advisers, training managers in conducting career discussions, implementing career planning seminars for employees, designing and implementing career components for special populations (executives, minorities, etc.), advising top management on how the organizational structure and culture are affecting employee productivity, and recommending organizational change efforts. The responsibilities assigned depend on the vision for the position(s) and the type of person(s) hired. Career counselors, like managers and other professionals, vary greatly in what they can do.

How many employees do we expect to be served? To anticipate the amount of service to be delivered, many assumptions have to be made. Consider this hypothetical example: All employees are in one location. The counselor is supported by a career center and a secretary who is also trained to assist employees in using the center. No other responsibilities are assigned, although the counselor briefly visits career planning seminars and new employee orientation sessions to explain the counseling program. The turnover rate in the organization is under 20 percent. About one in twenty employees seek counseling assistance each year, and their problems can be handled in an average of two or three hours. In this situation the counselor probably could serve an organization with 2,000 to 4,000 employees, seeing two to four new cases weekly. Scheduling problems, time for professional development, being out of the office for seminars and orientation sessions, conferences with supervisors, and other miscellaneous activities would keep the actual amount of time available for counseling to about 20 to 25 hours per week.

What salary and benefits will be offered? Salary and benefits packages vary greatly according to geographical region and responsibilities assigned. Investigating what counselors with similar training are paid in college and university counseling centers or in career planning and placement centers in the area may provide some ideas. However, these jobs are more secure, may carry excellent benefits, and probably are less demanding. Consequently, the salary range may need to be as much as 25 percent higher. The salary will need to be at least equal to that of other human resource staff with similar educational credentials and experience in the organization.

MOST COMMON APPROACHES TO CAREER COUNSELING

Career counseling can be approached in many ways and, according to the approach and style used can give quite different results. For example, one counselor using the trait-factor model (testing based) may merely test the employee, explain the results, and perhaps make a recommendation for a career option to explore or an educational program to undertake. Another counselor, using the same test, may spend considerable time in eliciting the employee's reactions to the test results, comparing them to other data about the employee, and assisting the employee in summarizing the personal meaning for total life planning. Time may then be spent in carefully outlining a detailed career plan that takes into account work organization and family realities. The latter style is more likely to result in employee commitment to a plan of action.

The three most common approaches to career counseling are the trait-factor (testing based), client-centered (reflective listening with guided problem solving), and the behavioral (analysis of and training in behavioral changes needed). Within each of these models, a counseling style can vary considerably.

Crites's (1981) work on career counseling may be extremely helpful in understanding these models, if you are an experienced career counselor. It lacks sufficient examples, however, for the novice to get a clear picture of the counseling activities involved. Also, it provides a summary of the literature; and counseling models, like management theories, may be quite different in practice from what has been written about them. In much of the discussion that follows, portions of Crites's book have been adapted for use in describing counseling with employees.

These approaches are distinguished from career advising primarily by the more intimate, trusting, open, and intense relationships that are developed and managed by trained counselors. Advising (discussed in Chapter 5) is less complex, more common sense, and rational.

❦ *Trait-Factor Approach*

The basic assumptions of the trait-factor approach *(testing and career information based, rational decision model*) were formulated by Frank Parsons, a pioneer in career guidance, in the early part of this century. They are simple. First, individuals have *traits* that can be identified and described. Second, jobs have *factors* that can be identified and described. Third, traits and factors can be *matched*; "round holes" can be found for "round pegs" (Crites, 1981). Unfortunately, this approach has fed into the incorrect stereotype most people seem to have about career counseling. They expect to leave counseling with a "scientific" answer to the question of what career option is right for them and to do this within a short, specified period of time, probably not to exceed two or three days of testing and test interpretation (preferably much less). Some managers who refer employees to career counseling may expect something similar.

An approach based on testing and career information can be useful, however. A good counselor can help employees see how unrealistic such stereotypical thinking is and use the trait-factor approach to meet some real needs.

Needs met: The major need the trait-factor approach meets is that of giving employees and managers no surprises in the methodology used. It provides something tangible to take away from the counseling experience. Unless used by a highly skilled counselor, this method may also allow employees to avoid dealing with emotional issues that may be involved in career decision making. It may satisfy their desire to intellectualize as a way of avoiding deeper issues. It can, however, if done well, provide a stimulus for quickly getting into deep issues that the employee may take longer to raise through other approaches.

Results desired: When it is successful, the trait-factor approach leads to at least five important positive consequences:

1. Employees are able to describe their personality dynamics, values, abilities, interests, and aptitudes in relation to the type of work roles in which they can be productive and find satisfaction, including their desired balance of work and other life roles.
2. Employees learn decision-making skills and become aware of their own preferred decision style so that they make and implement realistic choices about work roles and career plans.
3. Employees can state their career plans. Depending on the personalities involved, they range from highly detailed, time-phased plans with tangible milestones to highly flexible, open-ended plans for more creative employees.
4. Employees are confident in their decisions and directions and assume responsibility for their careers.
5. Employees know where to find the resources and support they need and how to get them.

Roles of counselor and client: In this testing-based approach, the counselor is more of an authority figure than in other approaches. The process is likely to be more structured, particularly in its early stages, with the counselor directing the process quite explicitly. The counselor usually takes responsibility for making sense of a great deal of data, explaining the data to the employee, and ensuring that the data are understood. The counselor may also ask questions to get additional personal information. The counselor may make a diagnosis of the difficulties involved in the career, explain the problem perspective, and talk it through in order to verify that the diagnosis is accurate. The counselor is likely to suggest a course of action for alleviating the problem and to offer help in making plans to implement the activities involved (adapted from Crites, 1981).*

At first, the client (employee) is likely to be dependent on the counselor, doing what the expert suggests, learning from a teacher. By the end of the process, the roles will have shifted, so that the employee assumes responsibility for career planning and the counselor becomes a resource person.

Brief narrative of activities involved: When employees make contact with the counselor, he or she talks briefly with them and explains the process involved. Together they decide whether the assistance needed involves getting help about career decision making and planning. (Such concerns as getting help with handling a grievance or making a job change to an already chosen position

*Grateful acknowledgement is made for permission from McGraw-Hill to use in Chapter 4 material adapted from Crites, John D., *Career Counseling: Models, Methods, and Materials*, New York: McGraw-Hill, 1981.

are referred to other human resource personnel.) The counselor assures the employee that the process should be helpful, and schedules times for testing and test interpretation. The counselor may also obtain permission from the employee to gather other information from organizational records.

The counselor may either administer or supervise the administration of the tests. Other information is gathered as needed. Then all of it is analyzed and summarized into formats such as profiles and narrative reports that can be presented to the employee. The counselor makes a tentative diagnosis to discuss with the employee (adapted from Crites, 1981).

During one or more test interpretation sessions, the employee hears and verifies data. Discrepancies between what the employee expected and the actual results are carefully discussed to ensure that the data are accurate and to try to get the employee to change self-perceptions when needed. The counselor explores with the employee possible personal meanings of the data. Together they identify career problems and discuss steps that could lead to their resolution. The employee is assisted in making a decision regarding a course of action (adapted from Crites, 1981).

Ideally, some type of follow-up is planned to help ensure that the employee is able to carry out the plan. At this point, techniques drawn from the behavioral approach may be incorporated into the more traditional testing model.

Variations: Variations involve the type of testing and data gathering done, the amount done, the number of techniques incorporated from other career counseling approaches, and the ways counseling is related to other career development system components. For example, if the goal is to have employees assume more responsibility in the process, the initial activities may involve a more client-centered approach to mutually clarify the problem, followed by employee participation in the selection of tests to be used. This variation requires a counselor with interviewing skills similar to those used by a therapist, as well as extensive knowledge of, and the availability of, a wide variety of tests. This combination of skills is difficult to find.

By contrast, the counseling model used may involve a standard set of tests and a group interpretation session. This session may be followed by referral to a career resource center for exploration of identified career options, or to a career planning seminar, or it may involve providing employees with information and developing discussion techniques for use in supervisory career discussions, or some combination of these activities. This simple model can be learned and executed well by a person with a master's degree in counseling that included a supervised career counseling practicum or internship. The training is needed, however, because lack of understanding of the psychometric properties of, and limitations of, such tests can result in inaccurate interpretations that are potentially damaging to employee mental health.

Materials and other resources needed and where to get them: The major resource needed, of course, is a trained counselor. People with degrees in counseling and with the business experience that gives them an understanding of the situations encountered by employees are difficult to find. It may also be difficult to find professional counselors who have completed internships in work settings. Consequently, you may want to hire a trained counselor and then provide opportunities for the person to get to know the company, much like new management trainees do, and to receive supervision by a counselor educator, especially during the early stages of getting the program established.

Initially, the counselor could be given responsibility for designing and piloting career planning seminars. The assistance of an advisory committee, drawn from different work levels in various divisions of the organization and composed of people with ample time to carefully pilot and evaluate the seminars, would be helpful. This guidance would help the counselor understand the organization and its employees. Later, the counselor could train others in human resource development to conduct the seminars, allowing more time for counseling activities.

Test materials, probably including computer software for scoring tests and producing summaries and/or profiles, as well as funding for having some tests scored externally, will be needed. One guide to these materials is *A Counselor's Guide to Career Assessment Instruments* (Kapes and Mastie 1988) published by the American Association for Counseling and Development (AACD). The American Psychological Association (APA) has established standards for such materials. Professional descriptions are given in *Tests in Print III* (1983), and critiques are provided in *The Ninth Mental Measurements Yearbook* (1985). Brochures from commercial publishers typically do not provide sufficient information for selecting tests. However, counselors can purchase samples for examination. Samples and technical manuals give the information needed for determining how well the instruments comply with APA standards. Also, publishers display their wares at national conventions of APA, AACD, and ASTD (American Society for Training and Development). Selection of tests and inventories should be done by an experienced counselor or psychologist.

❦ *Client-Centered, Problem-Solving Approach*

The client-centered, problem-solving, approach is primarily based on the work of Carl Rogers (1942, 1961), as adapted by Robert Carkhuff (1979), or on the work of Gerard Egan (1990). Crites (1981) has provided a helpful overview, drawing heavily on the work of Patterson (1964), with references to the work of people who were adapting Rogers' theories during the 1940s and 1950s.

Again, it is helpful to remember that the literature does not always closely describe actual practice. The activities involved are too complex to capture easily; individual counselors impose their own styles, even when they are attempting to follow a model.

This approach also has a simplistic stereotype: The counselor does nothing except repeat what is heard or merely says "UmHum" while the employee (client) solves his or her own problems by talking them through. In reality, in the client-centered approach, the counselor comes to understand thoroughly what is going on with the employee. He or she captures the essence of the feelings and meanings that are at the root of the problem and assists the employee to become aware of those dimensions and to define the problem in a way that permits a solution. The counselor then leads the employee through a decision-making, or problem solving, process.

Needs met: The primary individual need met with this approach is dealing with a career issue in a highly personal way and bringing the emotions involved to the surface. This approach may be appropriate if a need exists to identify resistance to implementing a career plan. From the organizational viewpoint, the main need met is that of removing personal blocks to productivity and to self-development.

Results desired: Success involves either identifying the real problem and taking steps to resolve it or rethinking the problem to eliminate it. If the problem involves the need to have a career plan, then the results desired will be very similar to those outlined under the trait-factor approach. They will just be achieved differently. Most likely there will be less data on paper, although the employee may comprehend the problem more deeply. The employee may also have greater commitment to action, because the process is more personal.

Roles of the counselor and client: In the client-centered approach the counselor does not try to come across as an expert who can diagnose and suggest a remedy for a problem or concern. The employee is expected to be in charge of redirecting the focus of the discussion within broad parameters set by the type of open-ended questions or statements posed by the counselor. The counselor assumes almost no responsibility at all in the early stages except for accurately mirroring the feelings of the employee. Once the employee agrees that a clear problem has been defined and he or she can express it with conviction, the counselor then suggests steps in a problem-solving process and assists the employee in moving through them, but still in the employee's own way (adapted from Crites, 1981).

Brief narrative of activities involved: The client-centered approach depends heavily on reflective listening and other techniques for building an open, trusting relationship during the initial stages. The purpose is to lead the client into self-clarification (adapted from Crites, 1981). In our experience the original problem is modified in about two thirds of the cases. A "real problem" emerges. It may not be a career concern, although it was initially expressed that way, but it typically is interfering with productivity, satisfaction, or both in the workplace.

The client-centered approach is excellent for communicating that someone cares, which, in itself, is very powerful. The employee likely returns to work with more energy. Also, discovering the "real problem" and defining it in very personal terms makes it much clearer and, typically, leads immediately to thinking of ways to resolve it. Finally, just a chance to express the concern decreases anxiety. The employee is less preoccupied with it and can attend to work better (adapted from Crites, 1981).

In the later stages of this approach, if needed, employees receive assistance in making specific plans for solving problems. They consider ways of making changes to benefit both the organization and the individual, and specify alternative courses of action. The values associated with each option are clarified and weighed. The employee makes a choice and specifies the steps involved in achieving various objectives; target dates for achieving milestones are set. Finally, the counselor and employee set up a plan for periodically evaluating progress and modifying plans as needed (adapted from Crites, 1981).

Variations: One variation in this approach is to introduce testing at the point where test results may provide data that are needed in either clarifying the problem or in planning. Interestingly, however, because this approach is usually taken with either interpersonal conflict problem or with managerial, technical, and professional-level employees, the data needed can be provided by the employee. Variations in resources used by clients are the rule, because of the highly individualized problem definitions which emerge.

Materials and other resources needed and where to get them: In the client-centered approach to career counseling, the major resource is the career counselor, who has sufficient training and the type of personality that are needed. The person must be warm, accepting, and genuine. These qualities make all of the methods work better, but in this approach they are critical, because they are prerequisite for the employee to open up emotionally and feel safe enough to risk appearing incompetent and unworthy. The counselor needs to be in command of a large set of behaviors that encourage self-disclosure and in command of others that assist the employee to become very specific in planning the latter stages of the process.

❦ *Behavioral Approach*

The behavioral approach to career counseling is the newest one to appear. Its main appeal is that it focuses on defining problems in specific terms and in ways that lead to observable changes in behavior, whether the cause is seen as anxiety or as a learning problem, that is, the employee has learned inappropriate behavior or has not learned to perform a desired behavior (adapted from Crites, 1981). (Incidentally, no popular, inaccurate stereotype of this approach is known to us.)

Needs met: Some employees may find it difficult to relate to a counselor who reflects feelings; they may not be sure what is happening and may distrust the situation. They want to hear responses that sound more rational and that assure them that the process is leading to more specific corrective actions. They want tangible ways of tracking results. The behavioral approach provides all of these advantages. Yet it provides for highly individualized goal setting because the initial task of the counselor is to listen and to elicit information that helps clarify the problem and its context (adapted from Crites, 1981). Not only feelings, but also the dynamics of the situation are summarized. This activity communicates both caring and competence.

Results desired: Success is very much an individual affair. Specific tangible goals are set with each employee. Success is reaching these goals. If there is anxiety involved that interferes with decision making, success may be identified by lower scores on a test of anxiety as well as by the actual choice made. If the problem is lack of knowledge, success is learning what is needed. If the lack is decision-making skill, learning the skill represents success (adapted from Crites, 1981).

Roles of the counselor and the client: The counselor in this approach is a learning consultant, skilled in assisting an employee to analyze behavior and in designing learning experiences to overcome problems. The employee is in charge of making decisions and doing the learning. There is a close relationship, however, that helps to lessen the anxiety involved. This approach also makes the approval of the counselor a strong reinforcement for action (adapted from Crites, 1981).

Brief narrative of activities involved: Counseling may begin with the counselor being an empathetic listener. However, the behavioral career counselor may use additional techniques designed to quickly address the crucial issues.

Behaviorally oriented career counselors are particularly aware of stumbling blocks that keep employees from seeing problems as their own, and of facilitating forces that allow for clearly formulating goals. They are skilled in overcoming difficulties. For example, one typical case is the employee who wants a promotion but does not want to put out extra effort to get it. The problem can be viewed as an employee who needs to clarify values and to learn decision-making skills. When this is clarified, if the employee so desires, decision making can be taught. Typical techniques include social modeling, reinforcing responses that are part of appropriate decision making, and teaching the employee how to discriminate between misconceptions and realistic approaches to making and implementing career decisions (Crites 1981).

Employees who are highly anxious are unable to focus on goals and ways to achieve them. If anxiety is identified as the problem, the counselor uses techniques for anxiety reduction derived from learning theories, such things as desensitization, inhibitory conditioning, and counterconditioning (Crites 1981).

When the situation is clear, the counselor moves to help the employee clarify a desired goal, a different type of behavior that would help to solve the problem. If, for example, the employee is young and has very little self-awareness, an interest inventory may be used as a starting point for exploring career options that are likely to be of interest. However, little other testing may be used. The assumptions are that interests can be pursued at various levels of expertise and that the major need is for the person to learn how to gain information and to make decisions, two types of behavior that may be new. If the person knows what to do but is not doing it, however, then self-managed behavioral modification techniques need to be learned. We assume that in the great majority of cases when people are not doing something, they either do not know what to do or do not know how to do it.

In other cases, the individual may be getting some type of reward for nonperformance, and the task is to change the reward structure. Helping employees to understand the reward structure, how the environment influences their behavior, and the options they have for changing the environment and thus their own behavior all become the focus.

Variations: In behavioral career counseling there is considerable variety, because each case involves a problem that is defined differently, in terms worked out with the employee. Solutions are also highly individualized. Corrective actions draw upon the client's resources and are also varied.

Few counselors use a "pure" model or approach, however, and this one may be varied by combining parts of other approaches. There is nothing to rule out bringing in humanistic, therapeutic techniques—for example, when brainstorming alternative solutions to problems involving interpersonal relations, or when there is a need to clarify feelings before translating them into the type of problem statement needed.

Materials and other resources needed and where to get them: The major resource is the counselor. Finding a behavioral counselor may be difficult. The behavioral approach is not as popular as others, possibly because it seems so analytical and practical. Many counselors seem to prefer dealing with problems in terms of internal behavior dynamics and conflicts.

Materials for teaching decision making may be needed, and the counselor may have to create them especially for your setting by modifying others. Workbooks and textbooks for high school students, for example, may not be acceptable to adult employees.

Because teaching employees how to explore career information resources is frequently an important part of this approach, having a career center is highly desirable. Additionally, managers should be identified who are highly knowledgeable of the organization and willing to talk to employees seeking information. These managers become vital career resources for employees. They capture and pass on oral traditions as well as highly specific and hard to capture knowledge.

SITUATIONS REQUIRING THE USE OF OTHER APPROACHES

Most of the approaches to career counseling assume that clients come to the counselor when experiencing a problem. Consequently, the work is remedial in nature. Few people are so highly motivated about self-development that they seek the services of a career counselor in a more developmental approach. Top management in an organization, however, may realize that a more active posture on the part of the career development program is needed. The goal may be to prevent problems such as those that typically occur at midlife and at transition points. Career counseling approaches that work for these situations may need to be used, and probably involve matching a career counselor with a person offering a seminar focused on the anticipated changes facing employees. For example, all employees about to retire may be requested to attend certain seminars as much as five years in advance of retirement. A counselor provides backup assistance to employees who find that the seminar does not address all of their concerns.

Another situation in which the employee is not the initiator of counseling can arise if a manager is having difficulties with an employee. Some counselors may be tempted to answer a request from a manager to initiate a talk with an employee. A better approach probably involves considering the manager as the client and becoming a coach to the manager, who remains the one dealing directly with the employee. Using a career counselor in this way seems reasonable. Counselors may need to spend some time adapting their skills to this situation.

EVALUATION TECHNIQUES

Career counseling can be evaluated very easily in terms of employee reactions. Ask employees for self-reported behavior changes; ask managers for their perceptions of benefits to employees. You will get understandable and useful data. Organizational impacts are more difficult to assess, because they happen in small increments over a considerable period of time, perhaps several years. It is also difficult to separate the impact of a career counseling service from other aspects of the career development system and changes in the organizational culture created by changes in management approaches.

Employees using the service should be routinely asked to fill out a reaction sheet, a brief checklist such as that in Exhibit 4-2. Although there may be some benefit in anonymous responses, there is probably more to be gained by having the counselor briefly go over reactions with employees for clarification. In fact, showing reaction sheets to employees at the outset and explaining that they will be asked to complete one at appropriate points in the process may be helpful. Also, asking employees to give feedback at any time during the process when they are dissatisfied or feel uncomfortable is recommended. Some clients are not aware that they should give feedback when they are uncomfortable or dissatisfied; they see the counselor as an authority figure and do not think it proper to challenge the procedures.

Probably the most important evaluation is client self-reported behavior change or goal attainment. Clients should be shown the form in Exhibit 4-3 and asked if they are willing to complete one at a specified period of time following counseling, perhaps ten weeks later. They fill in the goals for question 1 and leave the form with the counselor. To increase the number of forms that are returned, have employees address an envelope to themselves, put a note to themselves on the form indicating they promised to return it, and put the form in the envelope.

Managers can be surveyed periodically regarding their perceptions of benefits that employees gain from career counseling. Confidentiality may be an issue, but if employees are willing to have their managers know that they

Exhibit 4-2
Reactions to Counseling Session

Instructions:

1. Please put a checkmark below to give your reactions to the counseling session. If you wish to explain anything, add a comment.
2. Talk over your reactions briefly with the counselor; they will be helpful in maintaining good counseling services.

1. How satisfied are you with your counseling at this point?

___ Highly satisfied
___ Satisfied
___ Somewhat dissatisfied
___ Very dissatisfied

Comment:

2. How valuable has the time spent in counseling been so far?

___ Very valuable
___ Valuable
___ Not very worthwhile
___ A total waste

Comment:

3. How clear do you feel that you are on what you want to accomplish in counseling?

___ Very clear
___ Fairly clear
___ Somewhat unclear
___ Very unclear

Comment:

4. Would you recommend this service to other people?

___ Definitely
___ Probably
___ Possibly not
___ Definitely not

Comment:

---

have been to see the counselor, managers can be surveyed regarding their perceptions of the impact of the program on employee performance and satisfaction. Having an advisory group of managers assist the counselor in designing

Exhibit 4-3
Follow-Up Report on Career Counseling Session

Instructions:

1. Please answer the questions below; it will take less than five minutes.
2. Return this form to the career counselor, at the address shown at the bottom, through interoffice mail.

---

1. About ten weeks ago you completed career counseling; at that time you set the following goals for yourself:
   *
   *
   *
   *
   *

   How well are you progressing toward these goals?

2. Have you made any changes as a result of the counseling?

   ____ Yes ____ No

   If yes, what?

3. What was the major thing accomplished by your going through counseling?

4. Do you need further counseling assistance at this point?

   ___ Yes ___ No

   Comment:

---

survey procedures is recommended in order to have a survey instrument and procedure that fit the organizational culture. This approach is also a good public relations activity, but it should not be used solely for that purpose; it must be done genuinely.

For Further Study

To learn more about career counseling the resources listed below are recommended for further study.

Crites, John O., *Career Counseling: Models, Methods, and Materials.* New York: McGraw-Hill, 1981. Crites describes various approaches by summarizing literature in a scholarly fashion. It is written for professional counselors and advanced graduate students in the counseling field. Because there are few examples, beginners in employee career development may have difficulty understanding it.

Gysbers, Norman, and Earl Moore, *Career Counseling*. Englewood Cliffs, N.J.: Prentice Hall, 1987. This book presents many good counseling techniques, drawing on a variety of sources in a scholarly manner, and includes a career counseling model. It is written for trained counselors or graduate students in counseling.

Schlossberg, Nancy, *Counseling Adults in Transition.* New York: Springer, 1984. This book is issue-oriented. It does present an adaptation of the Egan counseling model.

Yost, E. and M. Corbishley, *Career Counseling*. San Francisco: Jossey-Bass, 1987. The authors focus on counseling for career choice. It is written for counselors of adolescents and young adults primarily.

CHAPTER 5

❦ ❦

Career Advising by Human Resources Staff

Jennifer, director of human resources, is talking with Ted, the career counselor. She says, "O.K. So far we are planning for our career system to include a career center, career planning seminars, career workbooks, and manager-employee career discussions. Do we have all the components we need? Will all of our employees have the career assistance they need?"

"Well," replies Ted, "some could still fall through the cracks. We probably also want to select some of our human resources staff to be trained to serve as career advisers."

❦ *Value*

Career advising by the human resources (HR) staff fills voids and takes advantage of opportunities. It solves problems that otherwise could be missed. For example, not all managers feel comfortable conducting career discussions with employees. Their subordinates may need career advising by HR staff. Or, career-planning seminar participants may want immediate, brief, informal discussions with the trainer. They may want to continue these discussions at greater length later with the trainer who understands the context in which the discussion started. If the organization has internal organization development specialists or human resource planners, these people are likely to get into discussions with career implications. If they have been trained in career advising, they will more effectively address the problems that are presented.

Chapter Organization

In this chapter you will find

1. Definitions of terms used in career advising by HR staff
2. An overview of career advising by HR staff
3. A description of how HR staff career advising fits into the larger career development system
4. A discussion of the decisions you will need to make as you design and implement this component
5. A method for creating models of career advising
6. An approach to training HR staff in the use of career advising models
7. Recommendations for coordinating career counseling, managerial career discussions, and career advising by HR staff
8. Recommended evaluation techniques
9. Resources for further study

Learning Objectives

In this chapter you will learn what career advising by HR staff is, how it differs from closely related functions, and how to design, implement, and evaluate it. After reading this chapter you will be able to

1. Define career advising done by HR staff
2. Differentiate it from related functions
3. Describe its place in the total career system
4. Explain how career advising models are created
5. Propose an approach to training HR staff in career advising
6. Coordinate HR staff career advising and related functions
7. Recommend methods of evaluating HR staff career advising
8. Become familiar with sources for further study

DEFINITIONS

Definitions in the area of HR staff career advising are somewhat ambiguous. Similarities exist in the activities concerned with career advising, but you will also find important and significant differences. Furthermore, you can expect to find disagreements about these terms among authorities in the field of career development and career counseling. We recommend strongly that you adopt a set of definitions for your organization. Frequent review of your own definitions with everyone involved will keep confusion to a minimum.

Career advising is a function that does not require professional training in counseling, but it is preferably performed by individuals trained to use career advising models. Career advising may be done by HR staff or a career center coordinator. Advising requires only good listening and problem-solving skills, along with relevant knowledge. Typically, it involves helping employees find and use resources for self-assessment, studying information on career and training options, using a decision-making process, formulating career plans, and implementing or revising those plans. It also includes referring some employees to career counseling, usually individuals who are unable to make progress in career planning for reasons they do not understand and those individuals who want psychological assessment.

A *career advising model* is a description of how one approaches career advising. The model can be very general, or it may be specifically designed for a particular type of adviser (HR staff member, manager, career center coordinator) working with a specific type of employee (executive, manager, minority white collar) with a given problem (feeling stuck in the job, wanting variety, needing more income). The best models are custom-designed within organizations. They are guides to assisting employees with their career planning in specific types of situations.

Career advisers can be trained by career counselors to develop and/or use career advising models. Advisers who are trained in specific models for approaching certain types of problems can do a better job than if they are operating only on "common sense."

Overview

HR staff career advising works best when carefully planned and when advisers are well trained. Good HR career advising can take many forms and produce a variety of desired results. Consequently, this chapter stresses the need for developing models of career advising and for training staff members in their use.

As presented in this chapter, the development of career advising models requires the staff to think through carefully the purposes and anticipated results, the type of employee to be served by a particular type of career advising, the characteristics and competencies of the adviser, the role, or stance, of the adviser, and the assumptions, limits, needed resources, possible problems, and the sequence of activities involved when working with a typical employee.

After considering the types of career advising that HR staff need to be able to do, the decisions that are made regarding how this component fits into the total career system, and the development of appropriate models, HR staff members will have a good idea of what training is necessary in order to execute the models well. Training may consist of learning additional information about the organization or new interpersonal skills. It may simply be practicing the models, trying them in real situations, and critiquing results.

HR staff career advising is one component in the total system. It should be coordinated with career counseling, advising done in the career center, and managerial career discussions. It also should be designed and conducted in such a way as to support the other functions in the career system.

HR Staff Career Advising in the Larger Career Development System

To get a general idea of how HR staff career advising supports and fits in with other career system components, assume that your total, although not yet ideal, career system includes the following functions: tuition reimbursement, job posting, new employee orientation, career planning workshops, career counseling, a career center, and managerial career discussions. As part of the system, each employee is supposed to have a career plan, perhaps called an individual development plan (IDP), on file in the human resource information system (HRIS) of the organization, a plan that is updated regularly. Frequency of the updating depends on the type of position the employee fills. Employees are responsible for updating. However, information is entered into the system by a manager, adviser, or counselor following managerial career discussions, career counseling, career advising in the career center, or HR staff career advising sessions. Employees have access to the IDPs in the computer, but cannot edit the files independently. The same approach is true for their managers, the career counselor, career center adviser, and HR staff members.

New employee orientation workshops, managerial career discussions, job posting, and the presence of the career center with its regular publicity encourage many employees to think about their careers. They encounter HR staff members periodically in the course of normal events. They ask career-related questions. HR staff members can then suggest other resources or can decide that a more extended discussion is needed and schedule a career advising session.

Such activities represent minimal involvement, and there are other, more complex, ways in which HR staff career advising sessions may evolve. Ideally, someone in HR should monitor employee records in the HRIS. Employees whose IDPs have not been updated on schedule should be contacted and encouraged to initiate a career discussion with their manager or to visit the career center. If they have not done so after a certain period, they are asked to come in for a career advising session with a HR staff member.

The models for HR staff–initiated career advising are somewhat different from those used when employees initiate the process. The role of the HR career adviser is different, more directive. The desired result is either to gain a commitment to career planning, jointly agree on a referral to a resource that can help the employee to identify and overcome resistance to career planning, or get the employee to acknowledge and accept the limitations on his or her career in the organization as a result of not updating the IDP. Limits on the employee's career may include such things as denied access to tuition reimbursement, training, or job change within the organization; limitations on pay increases; and performance reviews being limited to "satisfactory" until the IDP is updated.

Obviously, for all of these components to work well together and support each other, management from top to bottom must believe that employee development is important. Clear, consistent, well-enforced HR policies and procedures must be in place.

DECISIONS TO MAKE IN DESIGNING A CAREER ADVISING COMPONENT

In setting up an effective HR staff career advising function, a number of questions need to be answered.

Do we need HR staff career advising? The function may already exist to some degree. You may need to think in terms of enhancing or enlarging the component instead of creating something new. If it is already being done, probably a need exists. The answers to the by whom, when, why, and how questions regarding current activities may go a long way in clarifying what is needed.

What results do we want? The answer to this question is the foundation for evaluating the component and for refining it. Clear outcomes, kept in mind as the advising sessions unfold, keep advisers on track, too. In answering this question, it is important to include all types of outcomes for the organization, the employee, and the adviser. Some will be tangible; some intangible. Outcomes for the adviser are important because HR staff members have personal and professional needs, too. Examples of desired results are found in the discussion of models later in this chapter.

How do we staff the HR career advising function? Selection of advisers is important. The first step is determining criteria. At a minimum, staff members should be capable of quickly gaining credibility with employees; learning to communicate caring and understanding, while not assuming responsibility for employee problems; and learning and flexibly using career advising models.

What HR staff career advising models do we need, and how do we develop them? Before trying to answer this question, you will have specified needs and desired results, hopefully, through using basic needs assessment techniques and involving a career counselor in the process. The counselor can suggest approaches and activities that will address needs and achieve results.

Perhaps a few general, very brief intervention models requiring little more than basic communication skills and common-sense problem-solving skills on the part of the HR staff will do the job. Some needs may call for more detailed, longer interventions that also require specific, sophisticated advising skills and information. The discussion of models later in this chapter will help you to understand the range of possibilities.

What training is needed for staff? If you determine that brief, common-sense career advising models can achieve the desired results, training is relatively simple. Talk through the models with the HR career advisers and role-play them until everyone is comfortable and willing to try them. Later, meet to discuss results and to modify the models as needed. More sophisticated career advising models call for more elaborate training that is designed to guarantee that the staff will be able to execute the models well. Later in the chapter more detailed recommendations are made.

HR career advisers need training in basic communication skills similar to those used by managers in career discussions. Such skills include the ability to understand and respond with empathy to nonverbal clues, feelings, and meanings presented by employees. The most basic set of skills involves refraining from the types of responses that prevent open, caring discussions. These basic communication skills are outlined in Chapter 3, which deals with managerial career discussions.

How do we educate people in the organization as to what HR staff career advising is and how to use it? Educating people about HR staff career advising should be part of the total publicity package for the career system—announcements during orientation and career planning workshops, newsletter items, posters, and other media. It is important to ask what picture you want employees to imagine when they hear of HR career advising, and how that image can be communicated so that they remember it.

CREATING AND USING MODELS FOR THE CAREER ADVISING PROCESS

Needs met: Creating models is a first step in trying to understand and talk about the advising process. It is a way of developing professional skills. How we use models and the needs they meet change as we gain experience.

A beginner tries to decide which model is appropriate and then remember it, follow it within reason, evaluate his or her execution of it, and evaluate its usefulness. A veteran career adviser has developed the skill of thinking on several channels at once. When you reach that point, you will be aware of the processes you are using as you go through the advising experience. You will be able to evaluate the impact that your approaches are having, capable of changing them in keeping with the situation, and afterward able to summarize the strategies you used. At the same time, you will be able to listen closely and respond appropriately. You start with models, but with experience you may move beyond the need for them.

To say that models are not needed in the beginning, to say "just do it," denies or ignores the nuances and complexities of human interactions. Also, in many cases, a "just-do-it" approach leads to ineffectiveness that goes undetected, because you fail to evaluate and refine the processes you are using. Very few of us are intuitively excellent in such enterprises. So we need models to help us think and to refine professional skills.

Results desired: Successful career advising models are simple, powerful, and flexible–characteristics that make them useful. Flexibility and simplicity come from building models that provide only general guidelines. Details are worked out during training sessions; they vary for each adviser to some degree. Power comes from achieving a clear focus on desired outcomes and a means of achieving them. Success in model building sounds like a resounding "yes!" when advisers are asked, after trying a model, "Is it useful?"

Brief narrative of activities involved: To understand the process of creating career advising models, we first need to be aware of the contents of a model. To clarify our discussion, five examples will be used. (See Exhibits 5-1 through 5-5). Later, these examples will illustrate possible variations.

Exhibit 5-1 briefly describes a very general career advising model. An adaptation of one used by managers in a medium-sized bank, it is applicable to many situations (Marlowe 1985). Exhibit 5-2 is for use by an HR staff person assisting upper-level managers with career planning for possible promotion. It is an adaptation of one used with executives (Otte and Cully 1984). These two models are for quite different activities. Yet each has the same outline, and their content is similar.

Exhibit 5-1
General, Brief HR Career Advising Model

Purpose of model:	Provide a pattern for leading a brief career advising session.
Desired result(s)	
Organization:	Employee's plan is created and implemented.
Employee:	Assistance received; greater productivity long term; increased job satisfaction; absence of misunderstandings or unfounded expectations.
Adviser:	Sense of contributing to organizational objectives; satisfaction in mentoring.
Type of employee:	Any employee.
Type of adviser:	Any person wishing to assist the employee.
Stance of adviser:	Resource person for ideas; resource obtainer within limits.
Assumptions:	Employee has a career plan consistent with organizational objectives, is committed to implementing it, and is capable of implementing it with some assistance.
Limits:	Brief session, 15 to 30 minutes; one-shot, no commitments beyond executing follow-up actions mutually agreed on; if assumptions are not met, session is discontinued, and other resources are recommended; adviser restricts activities to stay comfortable and confident.
Resources needed:	None other than what adviser happens to have already at hand.
Brief scenario:	(1) Briefly set the stage. (2) Ask employee to outline his/her career plan. (3) Repeat plan back; clarify to satisfaction of employee. (4) Offer whatever specific assistance is possible.
Possible problems:	(1) Assumptions not met. (2) Employee wants more than adviser is willing to give. (3) Adviser becomes uncomfortable or lacks confidence.

Exhibit 5-2
HR Career Advising Model for Assisting Senior Managers

Purpose of model:	Provide an individualized approach for assisting upper-level managers in creating and implementing career plans.
Desired result(s) Organization:	Specific actions by the adviser and manager that contribute to creating and implementing a career plan for the manager.
Manager:	Assistance received; greater productivity long term; increased job satisfaction; absence of misunderstandings or unfounded expectations.
Adviser:	Sense of contributing to organizational objectives; satisfaction in mentoring.
Type of manager:	Managers one or two steps below executive level.
Type of adviser:	Experienced HR staff member, knowledgeable of organizational resources and procedures, credible with upper management.
Stance of adviser:	Consultant to manager, catalyst, resource person for ideas on career planning methods and materials.
Assumptions:	Manager will be basically honest with adviser.
Limits:	Adviser does not do things for the manager.
Resources needed:	Materials for manager to use or adapt when doing self-assessments, gathering information needed, and writing a career plan.
Brief scenario:	(1) Adviser makes an initial appointment to outline assistance that is available and to make verbal contract for working together. (2) Adviser periodical talks thereafter with manager in person or by telephone to assist in adapting and using an individualized career planning process that results in a written career plan. (3) Adviser and manager then schedule discussions to correspond to milestones in career plan and to revise plan periodically.
Possible problems:	(1) Manager lacks planning skills or other competencies. (2) Manager does not follow through on activities in career plan. (3) Manager does not disclose intentions sufficiently.

Exhibit 5-3
HR Career Advising Model for Clerical Employee Who "Wants More Challenge"

Purpose of model:	Provide an approach to identifying the employee's problem and planning a next step.
Desired result(s)	
Organization:	Employee commitment to quality, productivity.
Employee:	Increased job satisfaction, pride in work.
Adviser:	Satisfaction in following this model and in keeping responsibility with employee.
Type of employee:	Clerical, bored with job, almost any age.
Type of adviser:	Any HR staff person.
Stance of adviser:	Empathetic, warm, understanding, facilitator of problem identification/problem solving process.
Assumptions:	Employee may only want chance to be heard; may be presenting something "safe"; may or may not be willing to work on problem; must own the problem to make progress.
Limits:	Limit of one or two sessions of up to 30 minutes; adviser leaves all responsibility for action to employee except for some assistance in obtaining resources.
Resources needed:	List of referral sources for various types of employee problems.
Brief scenario:	(1) Explain purpose of discussion. (2) Ask employee to explain problem. (3) Listen actively; reflect feelings; summarize when appropriate; state limits if needed. (4) If problem is identified, ask employee to talk about possible options; ask if willing to consider other solutions; suggest solutions if possible, including using other help (accepting a referral); ask if employee can choose one option and act on it; assist in clarifying action steps. (5) If problem is not identified, state that; invite employee to think about it and talk later.
Possible problems:	(1) Employee tries to shift responsibility. (2) Adviser falls into "I must fix it" trap. (3) Problem does not have a potential solution.

Exhibit 5-4
HR Career Advising Model for Ambitious Young Professionals

Purpose of model:	Provide advising that encourages and assists young professionals in pursuing career goals related to organizational objectives.
Desired result(s)	
Organization:	Organizational objectives supported.
Employee:	Career plan supported and implemented.
Adviser:	Sense of contributing to organizational objectives; satisfaction in mentoring.
Type of employee:	Ambitious young professional-managerial or technical.
Type of adviser:	Experienced HR staff member; knowledgeable of organizational culture, resources and procedures; credible.
Stance of adviser:	Empathetic, warm, understanding, facilitator of problem identification / problem solving process, consultant, catalyst, resource person for ideas on career planning.
Assumptions:	Professional employee is highly motivated, learns quickly; has or can create, with minimal assistance, a career plan; will pursue activities that build a career.
Limits:	Adviser does not do things for the employee except to assist in securing resources; if adviser encounters issues that suggest counseling, employee is referred.
Resources needed:	A list of career planning materials available within the organization or which can be purchased; list of referral sources including career counselor(s); information about the organization.
Brief scenario:	(1) Clarify employee need through active listening and summarizing. (2) Discuss options and resources. (3) Clarify action steps. (4) Schedule follow-up discussion if needed. (5) Assist in securing resources as needed.
Possible problems:	(1) Assumptions are not met. (2) Adviser takes on too much responsibility.

Exhibit 5-5
HR Career Advising Model for Employee Overdue in Updating Individual Development Plan (IDP)

Purpose of model:	Provide an approach that secures compliance by employee in updating IDP.
Desired result(s) Organization:	At least: updated employee IDP on file. If possible: more motivated employee.
Employee:	At least: consequences of noncompliance avoided. If possible: renewed interest in job.
Adviser:	Satisfaction in accomplishing organizational objective and in following this model.
Type of employee:	Wide variation possible, but one who tends to drift along in job, who does not take the initiative in career planning.
Type of adviser:	Any HR staff member who has credibility with level of employee being seen.
Stance of adviser:	Tactfully and gently confrontational; patient but firm; representative of organization, responsible for insuring compliance with procedures.
Assumptions:	Employee's manager cannot do career discussion for legitimate reason; if employee does not respond to offer of assistance, employee's manager and other HR functions will allow natural consequences to take their course—e.g., no credit on performance review or inability to be matched with new projects.
Limits:	Session is continued only as long as employee seems to be cooperative.
Resources needed:	Information on organizational policies and procedures regarding IDPs; referral list.
Brief scenario:	(1) Contact employee's manager by telephone; try to get manager to handle it (if that is done, problem is solved). If impossible, (2) Contact employee by telephone; explain situation; offer assistance. (3) At first meeting, review policies and procedures for IDPs briefly. (4) Ask for employee's picture of the

(con't)

(con't)
situation. (5) Listen actively; reflect feelings; summarize when appropriate; state limits if needed. (6) If problem is identified, ask employee to talk about possible options; ask if willing to consider others; suggest others if possible, including using a referral source; ask if employee can choose an option and act on it; assist in clarifying action steps. (7) If problem is not identified, state that; indicate actions that you must take; allow employee to respond; recycle through parts of this process if employee decides to identify and work on problem.

Possible problems: (1) Information that IDP was not updated is incorrect. (2) Manager is uncooperative. (3) Employee is uncooperative.

When you examine the five models, you will see some similarities, but you will also see some of the possible variations in career advising. For example, one dimension for differences lies in the initiative. The initiative lies with the employee in three models: 5-1 (general model), 5-3 (the clerical employee who wants more challenge), and 5-4 (the ambitious professional). However, the HR staff person initiates contact with upper-level managers (model 5-2) and with employees who are overdue in updating their IDPs (model 5-5).

Scenarios and adviser stances, as they are described in the models, reflect this difference in initiative. When initiating, the adviser is more active in the beginning stages of the process and alternates between directing the process and active listening or providing suggestions. In the case of the delayed IDP update, the adviser is even prepared to be confrontational, if need be. When the employee initiates, however, the adviser remains in the active-listener and resource-person role.

Each model is aimed at achieving slightly different purposes and objectives, too: from gaining compliance (the IDP case) to being a sounding board (general model and bored clerical employee) to mentoring (assisting young professionals and senior managers with individualized career planning). The type of HR staff person who can be the career adviser differs somewhat in these models. For example, the general career advising model can be used with only minimal knowledge of the organization and very basic listening skills. By contrast, the model for assisting senior managers describes a process that requires a great deal of organizational knowledge and high-level consulting skills.

Remember that these five models only approximate reality. None has been designed to be followed exactly and completely in practice. Each situation is unique, and career advisers will respond appropriately. Additional variations and the complexity of the career advising process become clearer as advisers go through training. Each model summarizes its purpose, its desired results, the type of employee and adviser involved, the stance of the adviser, assumptions, limits, resources needed, a brief scenario of activities involved, and possible problems.

Purpose of model: Users of models need to know their intended purpose as a basis for understanding the rest of the model. People who are developing models need to clarify their purpose as the first step so that a context for further thinking is provided.

Desired results: Models in Exhibits 5-1 and 5-2 are for very different purposes, and their quite different desired organizational results help to indicate that fact. It might be possible, however, to have models with similar purposes but with different desired results. In that case, the meanings of the other items in the model would be understood differently in light of the results anticipated. Desired results also provide a basis for evaluating the model. They raise such questions as "Was something done that contributed to the employee implementing a career plan?" (Exhibit 5-1) or "Has the manager created a career plan and is she implementing it?" Then the why or why not can follow.

Type of employee: Differences in the way models are applied may be necessary, even if models are very similar, when they are used with different types of employees. The way adviser activities are executed may differ, as may the resources that are needed. Possibly even the type of adviser required to make the model work may change.

Type of adviser: Different types of career advising will require advisers with different characteristics and competencies. Personal characteristics of advisers affect the amount of credibility they have with employees. The competencies and aptitudes of the potential advisers affect the types of career advising that can be attempted. For example, finding staff who can use the model in Exhibit 5-1 may be easier than locating staff who can advise upper-level managers. Specifying the adviser characteristics that are required to achieve the purposes and desired outcomes is important. This information is used in selecting people for training in the model. Also, when creating models, the type of HR staff available may have implications for the way advising models are designed.

Stance of adviser: Stance refers to the way one stands; it is a metaphor for the role being filled by the adviser. Good career advising involves being very clear about the role one is filling. For example, is the adviser attempting to be an authority figure or a resource person, an empathetic listener or a teacher, a spokesperson for the organization or an advocate for the employee? Many such dimensions can be considered. Advisers who have thought through these issues and have a clear role in mind are likely to be more effective. They will be much more comfortable and therefore better able to think clearly and creatively. They will avoid attempting things not in keeping with the purpose of the model and will be less likely to experience burnout. They will tend to keep the responsibility with the employee, instead of being tempted to give answers or rescue people.

Assumptions: HR staff members like to help people; they may be tempted to try the impossible. Clarifying the assumptions that are being made helps the adviser to know who is an appropriate candidate for advising and what pitfalls to anticipate and avoid. Assumptions typically involve motivations and competencies of the employee, resources available, and what the employee brings into the advising session.

Limits: Limits may apply to various aspects of the advising process, such as time available, use of other resources, and restrictions on HR career adviser activities. Again, clarity in this area enhances effectiveness, as well as reducing adviser stress.

Resources needed: Resources may be materials that are used in advising such as information documents, human resources who make time and information available, funding for costs of training or tuition reimbursement, or any of the things available through a good career center (see Chapter 6).

Brief scenario: This section of the model briefly outlines the activities of the adviser and perhaps of the employee. It is the heart of the model. The description is very terse for the sake of simplicity. Details are worked out during training. The scenario needs to be brief and simple so that it is easily remembered.

Problems that may arise: This section of the model outlines potential problems. Again, details are worked out in training, as are potential solutions or coping actions.

Variations: The five models for HR career advising in this chapter suggest the many possibilities. Exhibits 5-1 and 5-2 are adapted from successful models. Exhibits 5-3, 5-4, and 5-5 are hypothetical, examples of "discussion-starter" models that might result from a needs assessment. A discussion of all five will help you understand what career advising is and how it is done. All of these models are used in our discussion of training. The five models differ considerably in what is required of a HR staff person to execute them well, although all are based on active-listening and problem-solving skills.

Materials and other resources needed and where to get them: As noted earlier, the fourth decision involved in designing a HR career advising component for a career system is "What HR career advising models do we need, and how do we develop them?" As a way of developing them, we recommend the seven steps shown in Exhibit 5-6. We know of no materials similar to the models provided in this chapter. However, these models are adapted from actual practice. This approach to developing and using advising models has been tested and found to work well. The major resource needed is a career counselor who can create models and train HR staff.

Training the HR Staff in the Use of Models

Needs met: Consistently effective career advising by HR staff does not happen by accident. Good performance in career advising, as in any other area, initially requires motivation and competence. Then you need to have feedback on performance, learning from experience, and satisfaction in doing the task.

Getting feedback may be difficult, because evaluation of the process of actual career advising is difficult, for several reasons. First, the managers of the HR staff advisers may not themselves know the processes well and therefore have difficulty evaluating advisers. Second, getting data is difficult unless employees are willing to have sessions tape-recorded or for HR managers to sit in on sessions. Regular training sessions overcome some of these problems.

Results desired: Training of HR staff in the creation and use of career advising models produces a number of desirable results. Organizational, employee, and HR staff objectives are met more completely. HR staff acquire more awareness of the career advising process and become more capable of improving it. They give more attention to results, increase their skills, develop greater confidence in their ability to do career advising, and improve their models for career advising.

Exhibit 5-6
Steps in Developing HR Career Advising Models

1. Secure management approval for engaging in this process.
2. Find a good career counselor, one who understands both career counseling and work organizations. You may have one already in your organization.
3. Have that person do a needs assessment. The result of the needs assessment should be a list of typical employee career problems, documentation supporting the existence of those problems and their impact on employees and the organization, and *tentative* career advising models designed to overcome the problems as much as possible.
4. Report to management; secure approval to continue the project.
5. Have the counselor train a group of HR staff who have volunteered to learn the skills of being career advisers. Participants can discuss the models, which are being proposed as a result of the needs assessment, and refine them in light of their experience and understanding of the employees and the organization.
6. As part of the training process, be sure to further critique and revise the models over a period of several months.
7. Thereafter periodically provide training to new HR staff who become career advisers and refresher training to veteran HR staff.

Brief narrative of activities involved in training:

1. *Identify a trainer.* You need a good career counselor who understands work organizations, can create prototype models after doing a needs assessment, and can direct experiential learning.
2. *Have trainer conduct needs assessment and develop prototypes of career advising models.* Using the models in this chapter, you can discuss with the trainer the format you wish to use. Don't expect perfection at this point. Models will be revised during training.
3. *Secure HR staff willing and able to be advisers.* After the prototype models are developed, you will have a better idea of the types of staff resources needed. If you are in a large organization, get recommendations from knowledgeable people; contact those people, explain the program being implemented, and explore their interests. You need people who want to be career advisers and who have good communication skills, particularly in listening, in order for the training to be successful. Selection of advisers is a key ingredient to making the program work and to making the training phase work well.

4. *Set up a series of training sessions.* Consult closely with the trainer in planning the training. See Exhibit 5-7 for samples of training agendas. This type of training must be spread out over time to allow for activities between training sessions. Potential difficulties include problems with making workable arrangements for tape recording and transcribing role plays, finding employees or HR staff to role-play, scheduling the role plays, and transcribing tapes.
5. *Schedule training.* Six to eight persons is a good size for a training class. Eight to ten HR career advisers per group is a maximum size. With more than ten people in the group, some of them will not be sufficiently involved in training delivered in the format we recommend. If you have 12 or more, schedule multiple groups. Otherwise, it will be difficult for all trainees to report on their role plays and to be critiqued.
6. *Conduct training.* Evaluate each session and revise in light of the needs of the group.

Exhibit 5-7
Sample Agendas for Training Sessions

Session # 1, Week 1: Getting Started (7 hours)

Session Objectives

1. Get acquainted; learn to be tactfully candid in the group.
2. Become familiar with models; revise and improve them.
3. Become committed to participating in experiential learning.
4. Establish plans for each group member to role-play a model and to tape-record, and to have it transcribed.

Sequence of Activities (breaks and lunch at appropriate times)

1. Share backgrounds, interest in doing career advising, etc., as a way of getting acquainted. (30 minutes)
2. Report on needs assessment by career counselor, including presentation of prototype models of career advising. (45 minutes)
3. Discuss models to clarify meanings of each section and to determine any special training needed. (45 minutes)
4. Role-play each model while group watches; discuss results to further clarify meanings of models and training needed. (2 hours)
5. Revise wording and substance of models in light of role plays and experience of advisers. (1 hour)

6. Identify general competencies required to perform career advising function well; plan the training needed in these competency areas. (30 minutes)
7. Discuss arrangements needed in order for each person to come prepared to the next training session—such things as ways of securing a person to be the "employee" in role plays, tape recorder, time and place, transcription, and copies. (15 minutes)
8. Critique the day. (15-30 minutes)

Session # 2, Week 2: Resource Identification and Planning (7 hours)

Session Objectives:

1. Continue getting acquainted, building trust and openness.
2. Identify resources needed in each model.
3. Plan to secure resources.
4. Gain skills in areas of general competency identified in first session.

Sequence of Activities (breaks and lunch at appropriate times)

1. Discuss problems in making arrangements to bring tape recordings and copies of transcriptions of a role play to the next session. (15 minutes)
2. Discuss resources that could be needed to support each model given various things that could happen in such advising sessions. (1 hour)
3. Formulate plans for securing needed resources. (15 minutes)
4. Train to build competencies identified in first session. (4 hours)
5. Critique the day. (15-30 minutes)

Session # 3, Week 3: Critiques of Role Plays (7 hours)

Session Objectives

1. Strengthen ability to tactfully give feedback.
2. Further identify competencies needed to use each model.
3. Improve skill and confidence in using models.

Sequence of Activities (breaks and lunch at appropriate times)

1. Discuss learning objectives and plan for the session. (15 minutes)
2. Share reactions to doing role playing, taping, and having the tapes transcribed. (30 minutes)
3. Go over ground rules for giving feedback. (15 minutes)

Feedback should be

a. Requested by the presenter, as specifically as possible.

b. Related to the improvement goals of the presenter.

c. Descriptive, not evaluative (not even compliments).

d. Supportive and tentatively stated.

e. Specific, behavioral.

f. Timely—specifically referring to the critique in progress, not to general behavior of the presenter.

4. Have a volunteer play tape of role play while group follows on transcript; discuss; use such techniques as

   a. Career adviser gives personal impressions of whether purpose of model and its objectives were achieved, asks group members for their impressions and for the evidence that they think supports them.

   b. Career adviser points out places that seemed to work well and things that need improvment; asks group members for impressions and for the evidence they think supports them.

   c. Career adviser lists areas in which improvement in performance will be attempted.

5. Continue these processes until at least half of the group members have presented their material and gotten reactions. (4-5 hours)

6. Critique the day. (15-30 minutes)

Session # 4, Week 4: Critiques of Role Plays (7 hours)

Note: Session is a continuation of week 3. You may think that this amount of training is too much. Our experience suggests that it is a bare minimum for really effective career advising.

Session Objectives

1. Improve ability to give tactful, honest feedback.

2. Further identify competencies needed to use each model.

3. Improve skill and confidence in using models.

Sequence of Activities (breaks and lunch at appropriate times)

1. Review learning objectives; discuss any changes needed in format for the day. (15 minutes)

2. Go over ground rules for giving feedback. (15 minutes)

Feedback should be

a. Requested by the presenter, as specifically as possible.

   b. Related to the improvement goals of the presenter.
   c. Descriptive, not evaluative (not even compliments).
   d. Supportive and tentatively stated.
   e. Specific, behavioral.
   f. Timely—specifically referring to the critique in progress, not to general behavior of the presenter.

3. Have a volunteer play tape of role play while group follows on transcript; discuss; use such techniques as
   a. Career adviser gives personal impressions of whether purpose of model and its objectives were achieved; asks group members for impressions and for the evidence that they think supports them.
   b. Career adviser points out places that seemed to work well and things that need improvment, asks group members for impressions and for the evidence they think supports them.
   c. Career adviser lists areas in which improvement in performance will be attempted.
4. Other volunteers go through same process until all have shared tape recordings and transcriptions. (5-6 hours)
5. Discuss and set dates to reassemble for discuss problems being encountered. (5-10 minutes)
6. Critique the day. (15-30 minutes)

Session # 5: 3 to 4 Months After Session # 4 (3 hours)

Session Objectives

1. Further identify competencies needed to use each model.
2. Improve skill and confidence in using models.
3. Strengthen ability to work as learning group.

Sequence of Activities

1. Discuss general reactions to doing career advising. (15-30 minutes)
2. Identify problems being experienced; for each problem, discuss possible causes; brainstorm potential solutions; role-play as needed. (1-2 hours)
3. Develop recommendations for improving HR staff career advising. (30-60 minutes)
4. Determine future training needs. (15-30 minutes)
5. Evaluate session. (15-30 minutes)

Variations: *More training in general competencies:* A number of variations are possible in this training, of course. In the sequence outlined above, for example, only the second session has time devoted to the general competencies identified in the first session. General competencies include such things as the following:

1. Listening and responding skills
2. Orally presenting information about career options, the work organization, and the career planning process
3. Being aware of personal reactions in the career advising situation
4. Developing insights and behaviors for keeping personal reactions from hindering the process
5. Revising career advising models in light of experience

Given sufficient need for training of this type, session 2 could be extended into extra days. Also, the process of identifying and then conducting training in general competencies could be incorporated into other training sessions.

Instructional techniques: The training sessions mention several training techniques, each chosen for a purpose. Comprehension of the models is achieved through demonstration role plays, followed by discussion. Skill in the use of the models is gained through tape recording role plays, transcribing them, and having the group discuss each one.

Other training techniques are needed. Listening and responding skills should be practiced in the traditional triad approach with a talker, a listener, and a coach. This practice can be within the context of the models or it could be based on whatever issues the talker wanted to use. Information resources can be studied in various ways. If the group members need to know more about the information resources available, for example, they can spend time in the career center. Either they can hear presentations explaining resources available at the center or they can individually work through some of the materials and report to each other. To help the career advisers learn more about the organization, resource speakers can be used; printed materials can be studied and discussed.

Additional experiential training: Sessions 3 and 4 in Exhibit 5-7 provide for each trainee to share a tape recording and transcript of just one role play. One may not be enough to develop the skills and the confidence needed. Having each trainee do a second role play and share it with the group would require adding two sessions, but it could also greatly increase skill levels.

Coordinating Managerial Career Discussions, Career Advising, and Career Counseling

The total career system in the organization works best when career advising by HR staff is coordinated well with other components of the career system. Especially important are close connections with managerial career discussions, career counseling, career planning seminars, and the career center. Informal approaches will probably work best. The most effective coordination will occur when one or more career counselors in the organization lead orientation and career planning seminars, train HR staff in career advising, and train managers for career discussions. This approach generates a common perspective and informal communication networks. Relationships that promote referrals will be formed.

If more formal efforts are needed, extended luncheons, where small groups are brought together, will promote genuine sharing of information and lessen the chances of the activity being seen as a bureaucratic exercise. These groups can include a career counselor, managers, HR staff, and career center staff. The announced purpose can be informal discussion of issues that emerge when working with employees and creating effective approaches to dealing with them. To enhance the learning process, luncheons could end with a quick statement from each person regarding the most valuable insight gained that day.

Evaluation Techniques

Evaluating career advising is very difficult, because good data are hard to get. Both the process and the results need to be studied. The best data for evaluating the advising process are audio- or videotapes that can be critiqued. The best data on results require longitudinal study of the career paths of advisees. In each case, data are difficult to get. Employees are reluctant to be recorded. Gathering follow-up data takes time and organization, both of which mean staff resources.

To determine if HR staff understand and use good processes, probably the most thorough and feasible approach is to role-play situations. Tape-record, transcribe, and critique the role plays, giving the person who was the adviser in the role play a great deal of control over how the critique is handled. This technique reduces anxiety, improves learning, and probably results in greater commitment to using good processes. A by-product is that everyone knows and accepts the levels of competence displayed.

We also recommend several techniques that are time efficient and provide some additional data: Have advisers make brief notes and keep files on each employee seen. One workable approach is for the adviser to ask the employee to complete a very brief reaction sheet (see Exhibit 5-8) at the end of each session. The adviser can look at it and ask the employee to elaborate a little, then make a few additional notes on the sheet. Assuming that a trusting and open relationship has been established with the employee, the adviser will get very helpful, immediate feedback. The written evaluation becomes a permanent record of results. All of the evaluation activity is part of the career advising session and a useful, clear way of terminating the session.

A simple way to get follow-up data is to have a form letter prepared; the employee can read it over, insert brief information, and put it in a self-addressed envelope to be mailed back to the career adviser after a period of a few months (see Exhibit 5-9). The authors' experience with this technique in other situations suggests that the response rate will be high. When letters are returned, follow-up phone calls can be made to as many as possible, thanking them for the information and asking for any elaboration that is needed.

Summary reports are then prepared from the responses to both the individual session reaction sheets and to the self-addressed letters. Preparing them need not be too time consuming.

Exhibit 5-8
Evaluation of Career Advising Session

Note: This form will be kept in a confidential file to be used only by your career adviser and your adviser's supervisor(s).

Please give your candid reactions below by checking the appropriate blanks. Then discuss your answers briefly with your adviser.

1. I __ did __ did not get from this career advising what I wanted.

2. I __ do __ do not recommend this career advising to other employees.

3. I __ do __ do not expect this career advising session to affect my work situation.

4. I __ do __ do not wish that something had been different in this career advising session. (If you do, please explain.)

Exhibit 5-9
Sample Self-Prepared, Self-Addressed Follow-Up Letter

Letter prepared on (date): ____________________

To (name of career adviser): ________________________

On the date above I spoke with you about my career situation, and I promised to respond to this letter after a period of time.

During our career advising session I decided to do the things outlined below. Checks to the right show results.

	Done	Not yet
1.____________________________	______	______
2.____________________________	______	______
3.____________________________	______	______
4.____________________________	______	______
5.____________________________	______	______

You may also be interested to know (comments):

Sincerely yours,

____

(Signature)

For Further Study

No resources can be suggested, because we know of nothing that has been written in this specific area other than the general ideas presented by Gutteridge and Otte (1983). The approach to HR career advising in this chapter was developed by the first author in cooperation with human resources personnel in a business setting. We hope that the models and the descriptions provided will get you started.

CHAPTER 6

❦ ❦

Career Centers

Jennifer, director of human resources, frowned slightly about halfway through the fourth meeting of the Career Development Task Force. Then she burst out, "If the other career system components are going to work, our employees will need to have ready access to some critical information. Most of them will want to know about career paths within our organization, and some of them will want to know about positions that are available elsewhere. All of them will need material on job search strategies, résumé preparation, and job interviewing."

The group members nodded agreement and quickly forgot for the moment that they were hammering out a career planning workshop. Suddenly they were wondering how open upper management would be with company information, what other resources were needed, where such information could be kept, who would manage it, and a host of other questions. They soon agreed that a career center should be developed simultaneously with the career planning workshop and decided to visit a couple of career centers to stimulate thinking about the career workshop.

❦ *Value*

A strategically located, well-publicized career center is another highly visible career system component. It calls attention to the total system and reminds people to nurture their career development.

Career center information is a timely, tangible service. It is delivered almost immediately upon request, represents much of what employees think they need, and is therefore likely to attract them. Then, once in the center, employees are introduced to self-paced exercises for self-discovery (which they are less likely to realize they need), encouraged to attend career planning workshops, and provided information on other available career services.

Career centers also provide opportunities for employees to follow up on career planning workshops or career discussions with managers. Information from the career center meets ongoing needs as employees implement their career plans.

❦ *Chapter Organization*

In this chapter you will find

1. Definitions of terms used in career centers
2. An overview of career center operations
3. A description of how career centers fit into the larger career development system
4. A discussion of the decisions you will need to make as you design and put into operation the career center
5. An overview of the planning needed to write a proposal and get approval for starting the center
6. Suggestions for staffing the center
7. Operating suggestions: what you need to do once you have approval from management and staff
8. Evaluation techniques
9. Resources for further study

❦ *Learning Objectives*

In this chapter you will learn the various characteristics of a good career center. You also will become aware of the multitude of possibilities that emerge from combining these elements in various ways. After reading this chapter you will be able to

1. Describe how career centers operate within career systems and explain the terms used
2. State the decisions that need to be made in your organization as it creates a career center

3. Write a career center proposal in which you describe and make a case for the type of center that is appropriate to your organization, specify needed information and equipment, and present a budget
4. Evaluate your center's operation
5. Continue your study of career centers

DEFINITIONS

Many of the terms used in discussing career centers are self-explanatory, others may mean different things in various organizations. For the purposes of this chapter, a few key terms and the way we use them are given.

A *career center* is a place provided by an organization where employees may go to study career information, career planning, and job search materials. Resources are typically provided through a variety of media. The center may also be the focal point for other career development activities. (It may be called by other names that include such words as information, resources, or development, as well as by more innovative titles. A *career development professional* is a person with formal training such as a master's degree in career development, counseling, or human resource development that has included coursework and supervised practice in assisting employees with their careers through a variety of approaches. A *coordinator* is responsible for the career center—a combination of manager and service provider, ideally a career development paraprofessional. (Many different titles are used for this position based upon organizational preferences.) A *paraprofessional* has no professional education in counseling or career development,but is a person who has been specifically trained in assisting employees to use the career center. He or she knows how to help employees clarify their needs, understands the resources available, has a good feel for the work organization, and can clearly explain the use of systems and equipment in the career center.

OVERVIEW

Career centers serving employees focus more on information about jobs within the organization than on general career information. Usually, though, some information on outside jobs is available. Centers vary a great deal in the types and amount of resources they provide and in the activities they sponsor. Many different combinations are possible. The following list of examples includes suggestions from Amico (1981), Bolles (1990), Hubbard and Hawke (1987), Moir (1981), and Stahl (1983).

Career Information Materials and Activities

- Organizational career paths
- Organizational job descriptions: hiring criteria, working hours, travel, pay ranges, and the like needed by employees in decision making
- Departmental or work unit information
- Computerized information on jobs inside and outside the organization

Training Information

- Local degree programs
- Workshops, seminars, and conferences

Career Planning Materials and Activities

- Self-assessment resources
  - Values clarification exercises
  - Personality inventories
  - Interest inventories
  - Transferable skills inventories
- Career planning books
  - Self-assessment exercises
  - Goal setting - information finding strategies
  - Action planning
- Computerized career decision-making programs

Job Search Materials and Activities

- Job search strategy guides and books
- Résumé preparation guides and books
- Interviewing guidelines
- Interview training
- Résumé preparation assistance

Career Centers in the Larger Career Development System

Career centers are a vital component in the larger career system. For purposes of discussion, assume that an organization has just under 1,000 mainly technical and professional employees, and that the total career system includes the following components:

Tuition reimbursement/support for training: The company reimburses full tuition for students earning a grade of "B" or better in college courses directly related to employees' current jobs or to jobs for which they are trying to qualify in the company if approved by their manager. Each manager also has a budget for his or her unit to send employees to training that is part of their career plan. Information on how this component works is provided in career planning workshops and is available in the career center.

***Job posting coordinated with human resource information system*:** The company has a computerized system that allows anyone to enter it, identify jobs open within the company, then access information regarding those jobs. The company's human resource information system (HRIS) is coordinated with job posting, so that whenever a job is entered as being open, the system automatically provides the manager of the work unit entering the information with names of persons who may be interested. Employees, with their manager's approval, may put their names in line for jobs after career plans are completed, usually near the end of their first year of employment. Semiannually, they may update their files through submitting information to an HR specialist who manages the system. Unit managers who have openings are supposed to notify interested employees personally through interoffice electronic mail.

Information on career paths in the organization, as well as related requirements and training, are in the career center. Veteran employees can use this information to supplement career discussions with managers.

Orientation/career planning workshops: All new employees attend a combined orientation session and career planning workshop beginning as soon as possible after they have become somewhat adjusted to the organization. The workshop is offered in half-day sessions; there are a total of six sessions. The career counselor leads these workshops.

Each employee tentatively specifies career goals, a career path within the company, and needed college courses or other training if possible. If employees cannot, they are asked to complete their planning when in career counseling. When tentative planning is completed, the information is summarized on an employee career plan form.

Training for career discussions: Employees are also trained through workshops to discuss their careers with their managers. Managers also attend workshops to learn their roles in career discussions with employees.

***Career counseling*:** The organization has a part-time professionally trained career counselor who also maintains a part-time private practice off site. The counselor reports to the director of HR. A full-time clerk is responsible for maintaining the career center, assisting employees in the use of the center, performing clerical duties for the counselor, and assisting the secretary to the director.

New hires are seen within their first six months on the job, briefly before career planning workshops (see Chapter 2), sometimes between workshop sessions, and afterward. Then the counselor carefully evaluates how well they have set tentative career goals and plans. When completed and confirmed, career plan data are entered into the HRIS by the counselor. Priority is given to those who were not able to complete career plans in the workshop. Having led the workshop, the counselor knows that they have special situations.

A major goal throughout is to make employees feel comfortable with taking additional time to complete career plans if needed. Careful work here pays off later. The HRIS entry for these employees is "career plan in process." After career plans are initially completed, employees are encouraged to talk with the counselor whenever they desire.

***Career advising by managers*:** Managers conduct career advising sessions with all employees at least every six months. Employees are expected to have attended a career planning workshop and a workshop on their role in career discussions, to have career plans confirmed by the counselor, and to have their career plans entered into the HRIS. After discussion of the career plans, approval is given at this time for tuition reimbursement and/or for attending training. Approvals are entered into the HRIS by the manager.

Managers attend workshops to learn their roles in career discussions, then hold career discussions with employees annually. Changes in career plans are put into the HRIS by managers and employees together when plans are changed.

***Career center*:** The company maintains a career center staffed by a full-time clerk (paraprofessional) and supervised by the career counselor. It supports the other components in a number of ways. Career planning workshops (see Chapter 2) are conducted in six, half-day sessions. Between sessions employees use the career center to prepare for upcoming sessions: Here are some examples:

- Use computerized career information and decision-making programs (see Chapter 8) to assess their values, aptitudes, interests, and personalities in relation to job families
- Pick up assessment instruments to be completed either there or at home, then returned for scoring for use in the career workshop or in counseling
- Examine information on career paths in the organization, job requirements for each position, and related schooling or training

- Explore information on opportunities for schooling or training related to the first couple of positions in a few career paths
- Assess the HRIS job posting system to determine positions currently available
- Study materials related to personal skills needed for advancement to new positions, such as résumé preparation, interviewing skills, and networking skills

Activities such as these assist employees in completing their career plans and in progressing within the company.

The organization explicitly encourages dissatisfied employees to look elsewhere. This set of policies and practices brings in more highly motivated people. The career center, therefore, includes materials to help those who want to seek employment outside the organization:

- Information on placement agencies
- Computerized information on types of employment in the state
- Department of Labor information on job openings
- Local public career reference resources, such as the public library
- Local technical and professional schooling in general, in addition to that related to jobs in the organization

DECISIONS TO MAKE IN DESIGNING A CAREER CENTER

Your organization will face a number of decisions when setting up and operating a career center. You need to have these issues in mind as you study other centers and write the proposal you will use to secure permission for starting a center.

These organizational decisions are *strategic* ones in the overall area of human resources management and development. Taken together, they answer the broad question: Does starting a career center fit well with our total human resources philosophy? Such decisions are very similar to those involved in other career development system components, career planning seminars, for example. Let's consider some of the questions that arise in this decision-making process.

How do we share with employees specific information on historical and/or planned career paths and specific jobs in the organization? The method by which information of this type is shared will create impressions and expectations. Specific and accurate information, publicly shared through a career center, as opposed to only being in the grapevine, can communicate that the organization is concerned about fairness and about giving employees opportunities to use their talents. There may also be very real risks involved in some situations, such as bringing to light old-boy networks that have just the opposite effect. The type of information and the method of sharing it must be consistent with the organization's culture to avoid creating problems and to achieve positive results. Carefully considering the impact that information dissemination strategies will have on employee attitudes is important.

Do we want to encourage employees who are unhappy here to search for jobs outside the organization? If yes, no problem here either. The career center can either provide helpful information or referrals. If no, there is still no problem, because most employees can understand this policy decision. The decision not to supply this information perhaps even makes the operation of the center a bit easier. See the For Further Study section at the end of this chapter for sources to which employees can be referred.

How do we want to staff the center? Centers work best when supervised by a career counselor or when they (at least) have a career counselor on call. Much of the work, however, can be handled by a trained paraprofessional. Train this person in greeting people and in directing them to the appropriate resources. Select a person who is both outgoing and a good listener. You may want to consider contracting with an outside career development firm to run the center. Another possibility is using part-time employees for career counseling and for peak periods of activity, such as after career planning seminars.

How do we get management support? You must always be asking how the work of the center can be evaluated and how the results can be communicated to management. Keeping the center alive and well requires continual "selling" so that people do not forget its benefits.

PLANNING A CAREER CENTER

A number of activities are involved in beginning a career center. This section gives an overview; useful details are provided in other sections.

Exhibit 6-1 presents the different steps in planning a career center. They are depicted in a Gantt chart, which shows estimated time lines for each activity. Time estimates assume that one professional is working half time on the center. Eleven planning activities are shown in the chart. Each is briefly discussed here.

Exhibit 6-1
Planning a Career Center: Activities and Estimated Time Required

	Weeks									
Activity	1	2	3	4	5	6	7	8	9	10
1.	--------	--------	--------							
2.		--------	--------							
3.		--------	--------	--------						
4.	--------	--------	--------							
5.				--------	--------	--------				
6.						--------	--------	--------		
7.						--------	--------	--------		
8.			--------	--------						
9.						--------	--------	--------		
10.						--------	--------	--------		
11.							--------	--------	--------	--------

Key to activities

Note: Dashed lines represent approximate starting and finishing times for the eleven start-up activities.

1. Develop a support network and study career centers.
2. Prepare a concept paper.
3. Set up an advisory committee.
4. Review other career development services.
5. Conduct a needs assessment.
6. Specify goals, objectives, and evaluation methods.
7. Specify types of resource materials and activities needed.
8. Locate and secure tentative approval for the use of appropriate space and equipment.
9. Prepare an initial and a typical ongoing budget.
10. Plan how you will move from proposal approval to full operation.
11. Write your final proposal and get it approved.

❦ *Develop a Support Network and Study Career Centers*

When approaching any new project, you need to have a vision of what you want to do. Ask yourself, *What do I think we need and why?*

To develop this vision, you need to do more than study this chapter. Visiting two or three existing career centers and talking with the people who designed them, those who operate them, and some of the users will be invaluable. You can probably locate centers in your area just by talking with members of your professional organization (American Association for Counseling and Development, American Society for Training and Development, Society for Human Resource Management, etc.). You may also find career centers in public libraries. Get to know people who work in these centers and who are willing to share ideas and to react to your first efforts in planning.

❦ *Prepare a Concept Paper*

Do I have enough management support to move ahead with the project? One good way to find out is to write a concept paper, or miniproposal, to request approval for a planning project. It can be just a few pages. Include very brief versions of most of the items that will be in the final detailed proposal. Indicate that this paper is very tentative, written just to give an idea of the general direction you want to investigate. You should find enough information in this chapter and in your network to write it. If you want to go beyond what is in this chapter, consult the resources for further learning.

Secure approval for the concept paper, perhaps from the person who has the authority to approve the funding you will eventually need. Clearly, you will want it from the level at which the total HRD budget is prepared. You want assurance that your detailed proposal will at least get a hearing.

❦ *Form an Advisory Committee*

As you move ahead in the planning project, you should be continually asking two questions and making decisions based on the answers: *Are my plans appropriate? How will the proposal be received?*

One good way to answer those questions is periodically to get reactions from an advisory committee. It should be composed of people willing to work, knowledgeable of employee and organizational needs, aware of both the hopes of senior management and the realities of resources available, seen as credible, willing to test ideas with colleagues, but also likely to support your leadership of the project.

The advisory group needs to be representative of the organization. Consult with your manager and other unit heads in developing a list of potential committee members. Beside each name, indicate what that person will bring to the committee. Carefully draft a letter inviting them to be on the advisory committee, which you are to chair. Have the invitation sent from the top executive who is sponsoring the project. Attach the concept paper and let the letter indicate that doing the planning and writing the final proposal have been approved.

Members of the advisory committee must be clear on their roles. Write a role description. During your initial (organizational) meeting, go over it with the committee members. Specify that they are to assist you in conducting a needs assessment, preparing a statement of career center goals and objectives, deciding on types of resource materials to be housed in the center, selecting activities to be conducted, getting reactions to ideas being considered, designing evaluation activities, and refining the detailed proposal.

Also, discuss with them what they see as inappropriate for them to do. Let them suggest the items. This strategy allows you to agree with them or to recommend that they take a bigger role than they may initially envision. It puts them in the position of setting their own limits early in the process, instead of your having to control them once they try to assume too much power. Your objective is to remain in control of your project while using their knowledge and judgment as fully as possible.

❦ *Review Other Career-Development Services*

A cluster of decisions will be made in answer to the question *How will the career center relate to other career development services and human resource systems?* You need to be aware of other career development and human resource services available to employees, for several reasons. By talking with others who provide services, learning what their objectives are, and rethinking services you may currently provide, you will be able to specify a tentative set of goals and objectives for the career center that are complementary to other services. You should be able to gain the support of other career development and human resource personnel in the process.

❦ *Design and Conduct a Needs Assessment*

If you have never conducted a needs assessment, you need to have tentative goals and objectives in mind. Then you can study needs assessment methods and talk with HRD colleagues who know needs assessment in order to generate a methodology that will work for your purposes.

The basic decision you are facing here is, of course, *What is needed? How do my own intuitions need to be refined*? Ideally, when you conduct the needs assessment, you will have in mind the general types of services that a career center can deliver and the needs filled by each of those services. This knowledge will enable you to develop both highly specific and open-ended questions for use either in focus groups (ad hoc committees), survey instruments, or both. You need to ask some open-ended questions so as not to restrict your data gathering to your preconceived notions. However, people frequently need specific questions as a stimulus to make them aware of some needs.

In the process of discussing the plan for conducting the needs assessment with your advisory committee, you'll also get into the question of *For whom is the center being designed?* You'll want to ensure that each target population's needs are assessed (you may find that some groups have more needs than others).

❦ *Specify Goals, Objectives, and Evaluation Methods*

Results of the needs assessment can be used in revising your tentative goals (global results desired) and objectives (more specific results desired under each goal). As you are revising them, plan your evaluation. You are deciding at this point *What will success look like?* If possible, state goals and objectives without dealing with constraints such as space or funding. Later you can set priorities based on resources available.

You may want to state several different types of goals and objectives, each of which ideally should be verifiable if attained. *Target population goals* may be stated in terms of reaching certain populations. *Objectives* are then written to specify serving certain percentages of various populations and subpopulations yearly for specific purposes. Populations may be broken down by geography, types of positions held, work units, or other criteria. You could aim to reach all new hires in their first year on the job to acquaint them with career paths in the organization, for example. Your evaluation would involve obtaining sufficient demographic data on employees using the center for specific purposes, in order to determine if your objectives were being met.

Acquainting new hires with career paths is an example of a type of a *knowledge goal.* There are probably other things you want new hires to know about the organization, possibly sooner than the end of their first year. The career resource center may become part of a new employee orientation program. You may want newcomers to be able to state certain things about the organization very soon after joining it, know where to find certain information as needed, and have target dates set for attending certain training.

Process goals can involve simply having employees do things with the assumption that they will benefit; processes can be open-ended, so that participants can set their own objectives. In these cases you set goals in terms of numbers of events, numbers of people attending, or percentages of populations. It is important to document benefits by having participants report whether or not they considered the activity worthwhile and what they got out of it. These evaluations can be summarized and reported to justify continuing the activities.

Document-based objectives can be stated. For example, "After going through our Computerized Career Planning (CCP) process, participants will have a realistic one and five-year career plan on their IDP (Individual Development Plan) form and will have entered relevant items into the Human Resource Information System (HRIS)." Then, if records are kept of individuals using the CCP, it should be easy to periodically check the HRIS to determine if information is being entered.

You can probably think of *skill and attitude objectives* that would be part of broader *competency goals*, such as improving decision-making skills. The more carefully you think through goals and objectives, along with evaluation methods, the more clearly you will be able to visualize your center operations and plan your work.

Once evaluation methods for specific objectives have been determined, you need to decide how your total evaluation system will work. Ask yourself what types of reports will be made to whom, when, and how. Ask yourself what decisions these persons will be making and what will be their basis for those decisions.

Have a "grand opening" with a party atmosphere to call attention to the center. Then create other special occasions to ensure that key decision makers visit the career resource center at least yearly. While they are there, give them an informal verbal report and hand them a more detailed written report as they leave. To remember you and the work you are doing, they need visual images and sensory memories of the place. They also need to know that you are documenting results.

❦ *Specify Resource Materials and Activities Needed*

At this point you are ready to decide *What resources and activities do we want to have in the center?* At the same time, you probably need to decide about what space and funding will be needed. This issue is discussed later in this chapter. If space and funding won't be a problem, consider materials and activities first. If you think they are problematic, you may want to investigate these constraints first, keeping them in mind as you choose resources and activities.

Remember for almost any goal or objective, there will be alternative ways of achieving it. For example, in acquainting new hires with career paths, you can provide diagrams such as organizational charts as handouts or as wall charts; show them videotaped interviews with actual employees, describing how they got where they are; have them interview older employees in person; ask the experienced employees to speak to groups at lunch; or provide brief written biographies of actual and hypothetical employees, both present and future. In each case, there are likely to be advantages and disadvantages, constraints and opportunities, related to your particular situation.

Ideas for types of informational materials and equipment needed are discussed in the section on operating the career center.

❦ *Locate and Secure Tentative Approval for the Use of Space and Equipment.*

Each approach to attaining goals also involves various configurations of equipment, as well as different types of space and funding. Ideally, first you determine goals and objectives, then determine resources and activities needed to reach those goals, next create a vision of how it all fits together, and finally specify space, equipment, and funding requirements.

We hope your situation is ideal. If not, you may need very early in your total process to tentatively secure space and funding for equipment and supplies based on estimates. Your visits to other centers and your discussions with directors of those centers should give you general ideas of what you will want. At some point you will have to decide *How do I get approval for space and funding?* Justifying your first requests by saying that they are based on what you have seen being done in similar organizations is about as good as you can do. It may be easier for decision makers to understand that type of presentation, as opposed to detailed lists of anticipated activities and related costs.

In your visits to other career centers, notice the amount of space involved. You may find that a center can operate in a space as small as ten feet by twelve feet. It might have a small round conference table or a desk for the resource person to use with employees, four or five workstations organized around different themes, a couple of small study areas, and a few racks for materials. Larger centers can be as big as thirty feet by forty feet or larger, with storage closets nearby. Such centers will have more work and study stations, a larger variety of materials displayed, perhaps a conference table, and probably a sofa and waiting area.

You want space that is accessible, where there is a great deal of traffic already—near a library, a computer center, a training center, or other activity hub, perhaps even a cafeteria. (Be sure to check noise levels, though.)

❦ *Prepare an Initial and a Typical Ongoing Budget*

Another major decision is *What kind of budget do I need? How do I develop it?* You can prepare budgets "quick and dirty" or in detail. The easy way is to tell someone who currently operates a career center what you plan to do and ask them for a very rough estimate of start-up and operating costs. You can get separate estimates for such things as career information materials, equipment, supplies, and personnel. Or you can make detailed lists of initial and ongoing needs in such areas, determine actual costs, and then estimate a relatively accurate budget. Needs and costs will change, so this more careful approach may not be worth the effort. It may be necessary, however, in order to satisfy the people in your organization who approve the final proposal.

❦ *Plan How to Move from Proposal Approval to Full Operation*

People will be asking, *When will the center be open?* List, as best you can, the activities that will be involved in getting all of the resources you need, then getting the center operational once you have your proposal approved. Do a Gantt chart similar to the one in Exhibit 6-1 for planning activities. You will need to include such things as preparing the space; ordering equipment and supplies, then getting them organized; hiring and training staff; developing informational strategies and materials to publicize the center; planning publicity; and piloting certain processes.

❦ *Write the Final Proposal and Secure Approval*

After studying other career centers, talking with people who work in them, and developing your proposed budget, you should have enough ideas for a final proposal. A typical proposal will probably include the following sections:

- Title page
- Executive summary (separate page, one-half page)
- Need for center (results of needs assessment)
- Activities and target dates for getting it operational
- Goals and objectives (fairly general)
- Anticipated activities and results
- Plan for documenting and reporting results
- Staffing plan, including your qualifications and role
- Space utilization plan (location, diagram of center)
- Budget

STAFFING THE CENTER

❦ *Job Descriptions and Competencies Required*

As part of the proposal to seek approval for establishing the center, job descriptions are needed. Assuming that a counselor is involved either full or part time, and that a full-time center supervisor or coordinator is used, job descriptions something like those shown in Exhibits 6-2 and 6-3 are needed. Staffing is a key consideration. (See Chapter 4 for a discussion of the factors involved in hiring and managing a career counselor.)

❦ *Selecting a Career Center Coordinator*

The career center coordinator need not have professional training in counseling; neither is a college degree required. Yet, the coordinator will be coaching and advising employees from many levels in the organization, so more than a clerk is needed. The ideal solution seems to be to recruit a person from within the organization who has demonstrated the competencies outlined in Exhibit 6-3.

❦ *Managing the Career Center Coordinator*

Even an ideal person needs feedback on performance, however. That person will also need the assistance of a professional career counselor in setting directions and developing models for helping employees and operating the center.

The career counselor who supervises the center coordinator, needs to take the initiative in scheduling regular conferences, probably at least monthly, at the career center. Other conferences should be scheduled as needed, of course. Many career counselors may be tempted to say, "Tell me if you need help," and to wait for the center coordinator to take the initiative. Instead, it is the career counselor who needs to take the initiative and be more direct; supervision is not counseling. However, counseling skills should be used to hear deep concerns and to involve staff in collaborative problem solving.

The monthly conference should have a name suggesting that it is a team approach to problem solving and celebrating success. The tone should be one of expecting success, celebrating it, and, as a team, planning steps to ensure that it continues. The session should not be a dreaded performance review. It should also be a session of admitting problems, so as to find ways of solving them, not denying or avoiding them.

The coordinator should come to these sessions prepared to do such things as the following:

1. Skim through operating manuals indicating where procedures are still working well and where they need revision.
2. Present a summary of data on use of the center during the past month, comparing it with use the previous month, and with the same month the year before. (The monthly summaries can be collected into an annual report when needed.)
3. Based on feedback from employees and on research regarding informational resources that may be relevant, recommend to the career counselor the acquisition of new, replacement, or improved resources.
4. Report any problems or discomforts and, if possible, recommend several potential solutions. During these monthly sessions, the career counselor should jointly clarify with the center coordinator indicators of successful operation. These indicators should be both measurable objectives as well as types of "gut-level" feelings, answers to such questions as "How do you feel when something is not right, but you are not sure what?" or "How do you feel when things are really working well?" Part of the monthly stock-taking session should be attending to such indicators.
5. Give feedback to the counselor on how well he or she is supporting the center and the coordinator. This feedback needs to be based on clearly articulated, mutually defined expectations that are reasonable for the coordinator to have of the counselor. Feedback needs to go both ways.

The counselor should come prepared to listen and serve as a resource person, but he or she should also be ready to provide such structure as is needed to ensure that a positive, thorough discussion of activities and results is conducted. The stance of the counselor should be one of providing validation and commendation of successes, along with encouragement to continue a commitment to quality service. The counselor also should be very clear in communicating availability, as a team member to identify and solve problems.

OPERATING THE CAREER CENTER

❦ *Preparing the Site*

Once you know what types of information materials you intend to provide to employees, you can determine equipment needs and the site preparation needed. You may find it highly desirable to have an architect (assuming your organization has or retains one) to assist in designing the actual layout of the center. Involving an architect helps to ensure that the center will be attractive and that details will not be overlooked. The architect will need specifications:

Exhibit 6-2
Job Description for Counselor Role in Career Center

Note: This description assumes that a counselor is available on a part-time basis either because the person works with several career centers or has other duties.

Basic Description

The career counselor supports the career center by providing career counseling when requested to employees, leading career planning seminars, and supervising the work of the coordinator.

Responsibilities

1. Design and regularly conduct career planning seminars; evaluate and revise as needed.

2. Ensure that publicity for the career planning seminars is developed and disseminated.

3. When requested, provide career counseling to employees:

   a. Administer or supervise administration of individual assessment instruments; score or have scored; interpret results; assist employee to incorporate results into career plan.

   b. Assist employee to identify factors blocking career planning or implementation of career plans and to identify resources needed or behavioral changes needed in order to remove the blocking factors.

4. Meet regularly with the career center coordinator to review the activities in the center and to plan any modifications needed in center operation.

Competencies/Qualifications Needed

1. Minimum of master's degree in counseling or in related field with coursework and supervised practice in career development and career counseling.

2. Experience in working with employees as a manager, as a human resources specialist, or the equivalent is preferred. Depending on the size of the organization, it may be possible to find such a person internally. Some employees have been known to independently pursue counseling degrees because of personal interest and with the hope of finding a place to use the skills.

3. Specific training in use of the career interest inventories such as the *Strong Campbell Interest Inventory,* the *Self Directed Search*, or others and in the use of personality tests such as the *16 PF* or the *Myers-Briggs Type Indicator.*

4. Enough general training in testing (individual assessment) to have the competence to determine the other types of instruments that should be used with employees and the training needed to develop competence in their use.

Exhibit 6-3
Job Description for Career Center Coordinator

Basic Description

The career center coordinator operates the center under the supervision of the career counselor ensuring that employees receive the assistance they need or that they are referred to appropriate sources of help.

Responsibilities

1. Be in the center when it is open or arrange for other staffing through the career counselor.

2. Provide either assistance or referral service to employees who come to the center in keeping with procedures and guidelines developed jointly with the career counselor.

3. Maintain the physical facilities and informational resources so that employees are able to use the resources effectively in an attractive and inviting atmosphere.

4. Develop record systems jointly with the career counselor; keep all records current; and provide data summaries as requested by the career counselor.

5. Based on feedback from employees and on research regarding informational resources that may be relevant, recommend to the career counselor the acquisition of new, replacement, or improved resources on a regular basis.

6. When approved, order additional resources and then incorporate them into the collection.

7. As employees complete their work in the career center, give out the feedback form used to evaluate the center.

Competencies/Qualifications Needed

1. Experience in and an understanding of this organization and its employees or the equivalent.

2. Cordial, with good basic listening and other communication skills.

3. Ability to generate trust quickly when meeting an employee from any level in the organization for the first time.

4. Ability to develop with the career counselor models for coaching, advising, and referring; then to follow and/or modify those models effectively.

5. Willingness and ability to maintain physical facilities, informational resources, and career center records so that employees are able to use the resources effectively in an attractive and inviting atmosphere and use of the center can be well documented.

6. Willingness and ability to work flexibly within general guidelines, yet to assume responsibility in the absence of close, direct supervision.

types of activity areas and number of each, as well as equipment or furniture needed. Remember to consider such things as location of electrical outlets, data or phone lines for computers, and lighting. Your architect may have suggestions for colors, carpeting, and other things that contribute to an attractive center—one conducive to learning.

Your organization probably has a maintenance or physical plant or construction department that must be used to do the actual work of getting the site ready for equipment and materials to be put in place. They are likely to have a schedule of work and a set of priorities; you need to make contact with them in the early stages of your thinking to determine what they will need from you and when and what type of construction schedule you can expect.

❦ *Initially Obtaining Information Materials and Equipment*

As you visit other centers and talk with career center coordinators, consider the types of equipment and supplies needed. Ask who the best suppliers are and what problems, if any, they have had with equipment or materials. Make yourself a supply list that includes supply sources and all information needed to order specific items.

We recommend making videotapes or audiotapes of interviews with people in your organization. Or you may suggest that employees conduct information interviews; they provide a very relevant resource for specific company information. Exhibit 6-4 provides suggestions. For more details on company information interviews see Figler (1988, Chap. 9).

❦ *Guidelines for Operating the Career Center*

Once the center is open, you will need policies and procedures to guide daily operation. A number of major questions should be anticipated.

When will it be open? Working hours in the organization need to be considered. The career center should be as accessible as possible. If maintained by a single person, it may be possible to staff it with someone who comes in at midmorning, takes a late lunch, and works until after normal hours. This arrangement allows for it to be open during employee lunch hours and immediately after work.

To whom will it be open? You may want to allow use by families of employees when employee use is not heavy. Brochures describing how family members may use the center may catch attention when other material may not. The center can become a family benefit at little cost to the organization.

Exhibit 6-4
Guidelines for Gaining Information through Interviews

One of the most interesting sources of information about careers is "real people." However, conducting interviews is quite an art.

If you suggest to employees that they interview people as a source of career information, they will need training in conducting such interviews in order to do them skillfully and to be comfortable doing them. Give them this material. Then have the employees role-play interviews or practice with one another in a workshop situation. Providing video feedback is the ideal way of helping them become proficient.

Create interview forms developed from the "Topics and Questions" below. Prepare printed lists of the questions to be used; plan to share them with the people being interviewed. The questions are not listed in any particular order. Employees need to be familiar enough with the questions so that they can skip around as the interview itself suggests.

After asking one of the questions, they usually also need to ask one or more of the follow-up questions, such as

1. I'd like to know more about _______.
2. I'm not sure I know what you mean by _______.
3. Tell me more about _______.

TOPICS AND QUESTIONS

***The Work Itself*:**

What are your major duties, the things you do most?

What is a typical day or week like?

How much change is taking place in this field?

***Preparation*:**

What preparation do you recommend to a person wanting to get into a position like yours or into a position that leads to one like yours?

***Entry*:**

How do people get into a career in _______?

***People*:**

What are the people you work with like?

What are the people to whom you answer like?

What are the people who work for you like?

(con't)

Satisfactions:

What particular duties do you find most enjoyable?

What type of rewards or recognition do you get if you do well?

What things give you a sense of responsibility?

What things give you a sense of achievement?

What is the typical pay range in this field?

What opportunities do you have for personal growth?

Success:

What is required for success in your field?

Are there any qualifications for success that are unique to your field?

Decisions:

What type of decisions do you have to make?

Problems:

What kinds of problems do you deal with?

Advancement:

Where can you go from here if you want to get ahead?

What does it take to advance?

To what types of positions would you move?

After Hours:

What social opportunities and obligations go with the job?

What organizations are you required to join?

Status:

Is your career field respected in the community, and how much prestige goes with it?

Security:

How secure is your position and such positions generally?

Retirement:

What are typical retirement plans? How secure are they?

The center could be open to the public, for a fee, but the problems involved from an organizational perspective may be too complicated to make it feasible. Consider having on hand a list of public centers to which people may be referred—centers in community colleges, public libraries, or church-sponsored centers.

Do you need a standard "intake" procedure? A file on each user? Not having a standard way of meeting new people is risky. It really helps to get off to a good start with a new user if you have perfected a standard "intake" procedure, one that is brief but which ensures that needs are well identified. Recommendations for doing intakes are provided later in this chapter.

What is to be given away? People do like to leave with things in hand, yet expenses must be taken into account. You may want to consider keeping a small number of a variety of handouts on hand and duplicating as needed to replenish your supply. Large inventories run up costs. Consider providing order forms for books, videotapes, and other costly materials. Be sure that free materials are duplicated so as to bring credit to the center, to communicate a "first-class" operation when other people see them.

What do we do when we can't help? People will come in looking for a great many things. Have a list of services you offer (for your own reference, if not posted) and a list of referral sources. You may want to have a policy of assisting everyone regardless of whether you help or refer them out. What you learn through following up on such assistance builds your list of referral sources. Telephone the referred employees later and ask how it went.

If in an urban area with a United Way, you may be able to get a reference book from United Way that lists all of the free resources in the area. If referrals are made, it may be a good idea to have several sources for each type of help needed. This approach avoids any possibility of being accused of steering employees to friends for whatever personal benefit could be involved.

Another difficulty arises when several employees come in at once and only one staff person is available. You may lead a small group overview and then suggest that individuals or pairs do different things. You can establish an order for talking with them individually.

❦ *Intake: Opening a Career Center User File*

A standard "intake" procedure gets things off to a good start. Strive for a brief, but effective, one.

Brief narrative of activities involved in first visit of employee with simple needs to the career center: When a person enters the career center, and the specialist does not recognize her or him, it is appropriate to say something like, "Good morning. Welcome to the center. Have I worked with you before?" If the answer is yes, then there is a moment of getting reacquainted, and the specialist pulls the person's record form as a basis for communicating and for recording the visit. If the person says that she or he has not been there before, a discussion can begin with a lead such as

Adviser: *Tell me how you learned about the center.*

This lead is factual, a simple way to start, and very useful information is obtained. It helps the center coordinator know how to publicize the center in the future, for example. Also, it avoids making people feel that they need to have a "right" answer because it is in the form of a statement, not a question. A good rule is to communicate requests for information through such brief statements instead of asking questions.

If the person came for a very specific purpose, perhaps referred by the counselor to get and complete a particular career planning exercise, this fact will come out quickly. In that case, the career center coordinator can simply say, "Let me make a quick record of your visit," using a form similar to the one shown as Exhibit 6-5.

Before beginning to complete the form, however, the career center coordinator should explain that there is a policy of confidentiality. If employees are coming on their own time, their managers will not be informed of the visits. What employees do in the center will not be discussed with others by the center coordinator. However, some people will be a bit vague, perhaps saying that they came in hopes of getting a better job after hearing about the center from a friend or through a newsletter. The coordinator can then take out the employee record form, and begin with a statement such as

Adviser: *I can help you better if I know what is happening in your life that made you think of using the center.* (Pause)

This open-ended lead is aimed at getting information on the person's situation, instead of letting the person immediately ask for certain information that may or may not be what is most needed. The person's answers should be pursued to clarify the situation. Use open-ended probes such as, "Tell me a bit more about ..." or "I'm not clear on what you mean by...."

The center coordinator completes the employee record form as the person talks, rather than merely handing it to him or her to fill out. The information sheet should be considered a discussion guide for a "get-acquainted" interview that builds rapport, not merely paperwork used to start a file on the user.

Exhibit 6-5
Career Center Employee Record Form

Employee name____
Work telephone ________________ Work unit____________________

Date ________________ Purpose of visit ____________________

Activities undertaken ____________________________

Results____

Next steps planned________________________________

Date ________________ Purpose of visit ____________________

Activities undertaken ____________________________

Results____

Next steps planned________________________________

Date ________________ Purpose of visit ____________________

Activities undertaken ____________________________

Results____

Next steps planned________________________________

Adviser: *If you were to find here just what you needed, tell me how things would be different for you.*

This question is also aimed at gaining an understanding of the person's situation. Again, follow up leads may be needed to seek clarification.

By this time, the center coordinator is forming a picture of what may be needed. It may be possible to get more specific with the discussion by saying

Adviser: *Let me say back to you my understanding of your needs at this point.*

After summarizing the main points and getting either a confirmation that the situation is correctly understood or clarification, the coordinator can then say

Adviser: *It sounds as if what may be most helpful initially is for you to....*

Then some suggestions can be made. Expectations can be communicated. The person can be encouraged to explore and to come back with questions or to report results.

Brief narrative of activities involved in first visit of employee with more complex needs to the career center: When the situation is complex, the coordinator may recommend an appointment with the counselor. A trained counselor can further identify needs to be addressed and determine if the career center is sufficient to meet them. This referral process is smoother if the career coordinator makes all appointments for the counselor within certain time blocks and can schedule one while the employee is in the career center. If not, it is desirable to offer to let the employee phone the counselor's office from the career center.

Even if a referral is made, some suggestions can still be offered and the person helped to begin work. An easy way to assist such an employee is to say, "Let me show you what we have here and see if you find anything of interest that you want to work on in the meantime."

This approach has several advantages. It brings the discussion back to something tangible, gets the person moving around, and winds down what might have become a somewhat intense discussion. It also acquaints the person with the center. The employee may find something of interest or see something that he or she remembers later and mentions to a friend with a need.

Brief narrative of activities involved with employees on subsequent visits: When a person returns, the career center coordinator should make sure that he or she has the employee's name right. After an initial greeting, say something like, "Would it be helpful to talk about what you need today?" The person may say "No. I'm just going to pick up where I left off last time." In that case the coordinator can simply request that the employee let him or her know when the employee is done and how it went.

However, the repeat user may have an entirely new interest. In that case, the coordinator proceeds much as if the person were a first-time visitor.

Materials and other resources needed and where to get them: To make initial interviews work well, in addition to the resources actually available in the center, you will need the following four forms: career center employee record form, career problem checklist (optional), a filing system for record forms, and a log of career center coordinator activities. These items keep things organized. They are essential for problem identification with employees and for documenting activities of the center.

An example of an employee information record form is shown in Exhibit 6-5. It may or may not give you everything you need. A major function of this form is to provide a record to be used in documenting use of the center on a periodic basis. It should be designed after the evaluation process for the center is drafted. It should provide the information that will be needed for evaluation, nothing more. It is tempting to include items on the form because "we might want to look at that later." Resist the temptation. If you are not sure of how you will use it later, omit it in the interest of cutting out as much clerical work as possible.

A method of developing the career problem checklist (optional) was mentioned earlier, having an advisory committee do it. If you use the checklist, get it set up in a very attractive format before duplicating. Items like this one communicate a great deal to users, through format and appearance, about how important the activity is.

The checklist could have a lead statement followed by choices to check. If the lead is—"I want more information on:"—examples of some items that may be listed are: (1) ways of clarifying my interests and values, (2) training opportunities, (3) options for advancement, (4) other jobs that would use my abilities better, and (5) other jobs that would offer more variety. The "other jobs that would" could be a lead with subparts, as could some of the other items. An advisory committee can assist in developing a thorough and relevant list for your particular organization.

You need a very accessible filing system in order to be able to retrieve user information record forms easily. It helps to have a file folder for each user. Other information may be included. An alphabetical file of folders should be sufficient.

It is important to keep a log of career coordinator activities: who is seen, by name, and with amount of time used. You also need a record of the amount of time spent on other activities. Daily records are critical for preparing summaries.

EVALUATION TECHNIQUES

Evaluation involves reporting activities and results achieved through the career center. The following seven forms and types of reports are the basis for gathering and presenting the information needed to know if the center is operating well:

- Log of career center coordinator activities
- Monthly and yearly summaries of career center coordinator activities
- Career center employee record form
- Monthly and yearly summaries of employee use of career center and results
- Yearly summaries of resources available and changes from previous years
- Annual survey of employee satisfaction with career center
- Selected case studies of users

Summaries of coordinator activities are prepared from the daily logs of coordinator activities. Summaries of employee use and results achieved are prepared from the employee record form. Resources available must be inventoried at least yearly; quarterly is preferred. Data on employee satisfaction can be obtained through either a special survey of a sample of employees or through building items into total organizational surveys if those are periodically conducted. The career center coordinator can be alert to major impacts made on the lives of some employees and can ask permission to capture and share those stories as case studies.

FOR FURTHER STUDY

We recommend taking a few days to do a local analysis of community resources that will be useful referral sources for career information. Do this by actually visiting various places. At each one, determine the resources that are available. Then make a standard type of record of what you find either on a large card for a card file, on a page in a notebook, or on a computer file. Decide before you start your visits what medium you want to use to keep records and how you will make copies to give to employees.

You may find information potentially helpful to employees at local community colleges, technical schools, other higher education institutions, the largest nearby public library, or at private career counseling firms. At educational institutions look for counseling centers and/or career centers that serve adults from the community in addition to students. Look for materials there that you may want to put into your own career center as additional referral resources. Public libraries frequently have sections of materials similar to those found in career centers and may have reference materials that would be very infrequently used in your career center—making them not feasible to purchase.

Local paperback bookstores are also worth a visit. Large ones typically stock many books on various aspects of the job search as well as directories of employers. Telephone calls to placement firms or to the nearest state labor department office will also be helpful.

CHAPTER 7

❦ ❦

Career Planning Workbooks

"This career planning program looks to me like it's geared toward headquarters people. How can we provide employees in other locations the same kind of information?"

When this question arose at the planning meeting of the Career Development Task Force, Jim, the committee chair, was already prepared. "That, Mike, is exactly the reason that we have been discussing options for individual self-assessment and for providing information about work in this organization," he responded. "What we want to talk about today is designing a career planning workbook that will be available to all employees, but will be especially valuable for those people who can't easily get together for a workshop."

Career planning workbooks fill a genuine need in many career development programs. They offer alternative formats for accomplishing many of the same objectives as career planning workshops, and the format of these workbooks gives them unique value to certain employees.

❦ *Value*

Knowing how to develop, use, and evaluate career planning workbooks is valuable for anyone who has broad responsibilities for career development programs. These workbooks are a valuable alternative to other methods for delivering information and for providing self-assessment tools. They allow employees who are geographically separated and employees who, for other reasons, are not able to participate in career planning workshops access to the information of these workshops. Their self-paced format appeals to the learning styles of many people, and they are a cost-effective tool for disseminating information in a consistent format. Knowing how to design materials in an engaging, effective way, gaining insights into the decisions about the content and use of workbooks, and understanding the options available through workbooks are valuable tools for anyone responsible for career development programs.

❦ *Chapter Organization*

In this chapter you will find

1. Definitions of terms used in career planning workbooks
2. An overview of career workbooks
3. A description of how career planning workbooks fit with other components in a career development system
4. A discussion of five key decisions you should make about the use of workbooks
5. Sample contents from actual workbooks
6. Methods and materials for designing workbook modules for topics commonly found in career planning workshops
7. Evaluation techniques
8. Resources for further study

❦ *Learning Objectives*

In this chapter you will find design techniques that lead to effective workbooks, typical topics found in career planning workshops, and evaluation techniques for tracking results. You will also find samples of tables of contents from effective workbooks, as well as samples of materials used in each of the typical major content areas. After reading this chapter you will be able to

1. Identify the decisions you need to make to develop a career planning workbook
2. Describe the content typically included in career planning workbooks
3. Begin to develop materials that fit your content, audience, and goals
4. Design evaluation processes to help you track how your workbooks are being used and how effective they are
5. Know where to go for further information or study

DEFINITIONS

A *career planning workbook* is a printed guide that directs its users through a series of assessment exercises, models, discussions, guidelines, and other information to support career planning. These workbooks are often described as *self-paced*, because they allow the user to proceed as quickly, or as slowly, as he or she wishes. Even though career planning guides are *commercially* available and can be purchased at bookstores, the emphasis in this chapter will be on workbooks that are *custom-developed*, designed and produced to fit the special needs and goals of an organization and its career development efforts.

OVERVIEW

Organizations offer career planning workbooks for a variety of different reasons. Often they are used to supplement career planning workshops. In these cases the workbooks may be required "pre-work," thus allowing the entire group to begin the workshop "on the same foot" (i.e., with at least a minimum of shared information and preparation), and it reinforces the commitment of participants in the workshop. Other times, career planning workbooks may follow the workshop, as a means of ongoing support and learning.

Career planning workbooks are frequently used to provide a means for sharing information and supporting individual self assessment and career planning for employees who would find it difficult to attend a workshop. Employees in small offices, remote locations, or whose jobs require unusual working hours often use workbooks as their major tool for establishing career plans and goals and for preparing to talk with their managers about their careers.

Workbooks vary in length, format, and type of publication. Some are designed to be completed in a short time (two hours or less); others are intended to be used in small subsections, but require many hours (30 or more, if all activities are undertaken) to complete. The number of pages may range from as few as 25 to more than 100. Most workbooks have a lot of interactive material, allowing the user to fill in charts, complete quizzes, or respond to questions. Some also include a lot of information about how people develop, career types, stages, and so on. Most organizations that develop their own career planning workbooks include information describing the structure of the company and the type of work available within different parts of the business. Often workbooks are not published as "books" per se. Sometimes they are in three-ring binders or folders, enabling materials to be easily added or changed. Other times, they are bound with attractive covers and look more like a traditional book.

CAREER PLANNING WORKBOOKS IN THE LARGER CAREER DEVELOPMENT SYSTEM

Career planning workbooks are among the most versatile components of a career system because they can be designed to support virtually any other component. They can be a primary vehicle to disseminate information about the entire career system, or they can be more narrowly focused to serve specific functions within the system. Since they are printed documents, they offer a consistent approach to exploring careers and gathering pertinent information for career planning and development.

Two ways that workbooks support career planning workshops have already been pointed out–pre-work and follow-up. In addition, a career planning workbook may actually serve as the participant's materials for a career workshop. This ensures that all participants, whether they attend the workshop or whether they complete career planning individually at their own pace, cover the same material and receive the same information.

Career planning workbooks are valuable additions to a career center. Those available commercially and purchased for inclusion in the center offer useful insights, assessments, and information. Those developed specifically for an organization often provide introductory information about the company—its structure, types of work, goals, and the like. Workbooks provide good overviews for more complete information that may exist in the career center.

Sometimes employees who visit the career counselor or career adviser may be referred to a career workbook as part of the counseling or guidance process. Career planning workbooks can be used to provide a structured approach for assignments for the employee to complete between discussions with the counselor or career adviser. This helps the employee to demonstrate responsibility for planning and directing his or her career.

Career planning workbooks are valuable resources to support the manager-employee career discussion. Managers may encourage employees to complete the workbook, or selected sections, to help prepare for the discussion. Some workbooks even include a preparation guide to support this career discussion.

DECISIONS TO MAKE IN DESIGNING CAREER WORKBOOKS

Questions such as the ones addressed below are important when designing career workbooks. They represent basic decisions that need to be made as early as possible in the planning and development process.

What is the goal of the workbook? The goal of the workbook may be as specific as to provide self-assessment for career planning workshop participants, or as broad as to provide information and tools to help employees develop realistic career plans. The goal of the workbook may be to support other components, or it may be to serve as the major piece of information employees receive in the organization's career development efforts. Some career planning workbooks even have purposes that include being used in recruiting. Deciding on the goal of the workbook requires thinking through when and how it will be distributed, as well as what results you expect from its use.

Who is the target audience? Who will use the workbook? The workbook may be developed for all employees, or it may be directed toward a particular group of employees (field service personnel, internationally based employees, engineers). It may be intended for distribution within one division or segment of the organization, or it may be written so as to be appropriate for all parts of the business.

To what degree do you want the workbook to truly "stand alone?" If the workbook is to be used without access to a counselor, workshop, or other resource for assistance, it must include complete discussions for each exercise, as well as clear instructions and up-to-date information. On the other hand, if the user is expected to routinely have access to someone who can answer questions, participate in discussions, and make suggestions, the workbook can be written in a crisper, shorter style.

Do you have the resources to write and publish the book within the organization, or will a professional be hired to produce your book? You may have editorial assistance within the company. If so, you may well be able to produce your own high-quality workbook. Remember, though, that a project of this kind requires special skills and information. The writer should know about career planning and development and designing self-paced learning, as well as have the skills to write in a way that will engage your target group.

How will you update the workbook? This decision will dictate both the binding of the workbook and the type of information about the organization and its work options. If you want to include very specific information, but the information is subject to frequent change, you may choose a three-ring binder or folder over a saddle-stitched binding. Few organizations would risk publishing information such as organization charts with names for each position in a workbook that required full reprinting and binding to update.

All of these decisions will lead you to the choices about the format (loose-leaf or bound), the layout and design (size of pages, type, use of graphics, charts, pictures), the editorial style (fun? serious?), and reading level. Each of these decisions also has budget implications. It is wise to explore more than one option for publishing and then gather specifications and price quotations for each. In this way your choices become clearer, and you can be more conscious of the trade-offs involved.

TYPICAL CONTENTS OF A CAREER PLANNING WORKBOOK

Since the goals and planned use of a workbook dictate the content appropriate for that book, there is no "correct" content for a workbook. There are, however, some "typical" content areas. Like career planning workshops, virtually all workbooks contain several common elements: introduction (setting the stage, outlining roles and responsibilities); individual self-assessment; information about the organization and work options available; goal setting (both long and short term) and decision making; resources available to support employee career development; and establishing and implementing a career plan. Often workbooks include forms to complete for analyzing career options and, sometimes, for preparing for a career discussion with a manager. Sample tables of contents for career planning workbooks are presented in Exhibits 7-1 and 7-2.

Now that you have the big picture view of career workbooks, we will discuss how each of the major sections of these workbooks typically unfolds. Each section will present the needs (goals) met by this section, the desired results, and a description of the information and exercises that might be included. Some variations are offered that you might want to consider, as well as descriptions of materials or resources to help you prepare this for your organization.

❦ *Introduction: Setting the Stage*

The introductory section of career planning workbooks is designed to prepare the user for the material to come, to provide a brief introduction to the underlying philosophies and/or programs included in the organization's career development system, and to build support and enthusiasm for the program with the endorsement of a chief officer of the company.

Needs met: Introductory materials prepare the user of the workbook for what is to come. In effect, they set the stage for the information and activities that are to follow. They also prepare the user psychologically to anticipate what the results of using these materials will, and will not, be. Finally, the introduc-

Exhibit 7-1
Table of Contents
for Short Career Planning Workbook

tion is used to stress the organization's basic beliefs about career development and the appropriate roles for the company, for managers, and for employees in the career development process.

Desired results: The introductory section of the career planning workbook will be considered successful when it prepares users to move ahead in a positive, realistic frame of mind. The introductory materials should

1. Build the user's enthusiasm for participating in the program
2. Encourage the user to accept primary responsibility for managing his or her own career

Exhibit 7-2
Table of Contents
for Longer Career Planning Workbook

Chapter 1 - Getting Started
What Is Career Planning
Some Basic Terms
Plan Your Approach
Benefits and Risks
Career Planning Model
Career Development Philosophy
Career Development at Our Company
Looking Back and Looking Ahead

Chapter 2 - Taking a Snapshot Of Myself
Life Career Stages
Career Stages and Tasks
Career Life Line
Best Case/Worst Case
Sorting Out Work Values
Examining Successes
Career Anchors
Assessing Skills
Skills for the Future
Abracadabra
Self-Portrait
Looking Back and Looking Ahead

Chapter 3 - Finding a Job That Fits
Overview of Company
Career Opportunities and Career Movement
Descriptions Of Functional Units Within Company
Career Direction Options
Up Is Not the Only Way To Go
Looking Beyond the Current Job
Identifying Career Options
Developing a Career Path
The Career Information Interview
Looking Back and Looking Ahead

Chapter 4 - Charting Your Course
Reality Testing Your Perceptions
Documenting Your Contacts
Your Ideal Career
Goal Setting
Developing a Career Goal Statement
Career Decisions
Looking Back and Looking Ahead

Chapter 5 - Making Use of Career Development Resources
Individual Development Needs
Career Development Resources
Identifying Resources to Meet Your Needs
The Career Discussion
Career Enhancement Form
Looking Back and Looking Ahead

Chapter 6 - Overcoming Obstacles
Politics and Careers
Increasing Your Influence
Managing Career Plateaus
Developing a Career Support Network
Career Realities and Issues
Looking Back and Looking Ahead

Chapter 7 - Getting Moving
Maintaining Your Momentum
Committing to Next Steps
Looking Back and Looking Ahead
Evaluation

Career Planning Worksheet

Appendix: Organization Chart

From NCR employee career planning workbook, *Creating Value through Career Planning at NCR*, 1990. Used with permission.

3. Present realistic pictures of what can and cannot be expected from using the workbook
4. Explain the different roles involved in career development within the organization

Information and exercises frequently included: Often a career planning workbook is introduced by a letter from the president or other executive in the organization. This letter explains the goals of the workbook, describes how this fits with the employee development philosophy of the organization, and encourages the employee to participate fully and honestly in the process. Other parts of the introductory material elaborate on the philosophy and/or goals the organization has for employee development; outline the roles assigned to the individual, the organization, and managers; and help the employee explore both the benefits and risks of participating in career development activities.

If the workbook is to be a short one, these introductory materials may be limited to only a few pages. In longer workbooks, they may be given as many as 10 to 12 pages.

❦ *Self-Assessment: Evaluating Self*

This second major section of a career planning workbook serves the same purpose as the assessment modules of career planning workshops: to equip the employee with sufficient information about self to make career decisions that result in both success and satisfaction on the job. Just as in career planning workshops, these exercises focus on helping the individual answer such questions as "Who am I?" " What can I do well?" "What do I enjoy doing?"

Needs met: This section allows individuals to analyze themselves from a number of different perspectives. The result is the information required to make effective current and future career choices. Without this information, career planning is futile, as the employee lacks the needed data to make independent choices that will meet his or her needs.

Desired results: The self-assessment portion of the workbook can be considered successful when it provides employees with the information to begin answering such questions as

- What are my work skills?
- How can I gain the most satisfaction from my work?
- What are the most important work values for me?
- What are some trade-offs I am willing to make for my career?
- What trade-offs seem too costly to make?
- What does "success" mean to me?
- What do I need to be doing now to prepare myself for ongoing career satisfaction and success?

Self-assessment information and exercises frequently included: In many workbooks, self-assessment is the longest section of the book. Here you will find inventories and assessments to help the employee identify both strengths and development needs for the skills and knowledge needed for career success, as well as explore individual interests, prioritize values, and examine personal characteristics.

The assessments in this section of the career planning workbook may be created especially for the workbook, or you may prefer to use commercial assessment instruments. When off-the-shelf self assessment instruments are used, it is important to provide follow-up discussion and opportunities to integrate these results with other materials developed internally.

The following discussion of the types of assessments often included in career planning workbooks is not intended to be "ideal." Rather, it is an extended list to provide an overview of options to consider. Exhibits 7-3 through 7-5 present samples of self assessments from existing career planning workbooks.

An assessment of accomplishments asks the career planner to look back over the times in life that have been particularly satisfying and to examine these situations to identify themes useful for evaluating future options. Sometimes this exercise is left open–the participant is not given directions about how to select incidents. Other times, time frames are included, guiding the individual to select incidents beginning in school years and continuing up to the present.

Another tool for helping to identify what has contributed to both successes and low points in careers is the *career life line* activity. In this exercise, participants draw (or create with other materials) a line that represents the time of their career lives and show the relative high and low points along the line.

Sometimes career planners need to identify their own *life and career stage* in order to understand what they need to focus on to develop their careers. These stages have been defined in a number of slightly different ways. Two to consider are typical career challenges by chronological age (see Super 1975) and career tasks by number of years/developmental stage in the career (see Dalton and Thompson 1986).

Exercises to examine *work values* generally provide a list of possible values and ask the person completing the exercise to rate or rank each value. The result is a prioritized list of "what is important for me at work," which can be used to compare with what the current job offers, as well as to evaluate potential future options.

Lists of competencies, or work skills, are presented for the individual to evaluate. Often, these lists are rated twice by each person completing the exercise–once to evaluate how important the skill is for the individual's work and once to evaluate the individual's proficiency. Sometimes companion lists are available for either managers or others who know the individual well, providing a reality check for the self-assessment.

Exhibit 7-3
Sample Self-Assessment

Career Life Line: A good place to begin self-assessment is to summarize where you have been and where you are now in terms of your career. This can be done graphically by plotting the quality of your career at different time intervals on the chart below. We have all had "ups" and "downs" during our career; therefore, we would expect to see peaks and valleys in our graph rather than a straight line.

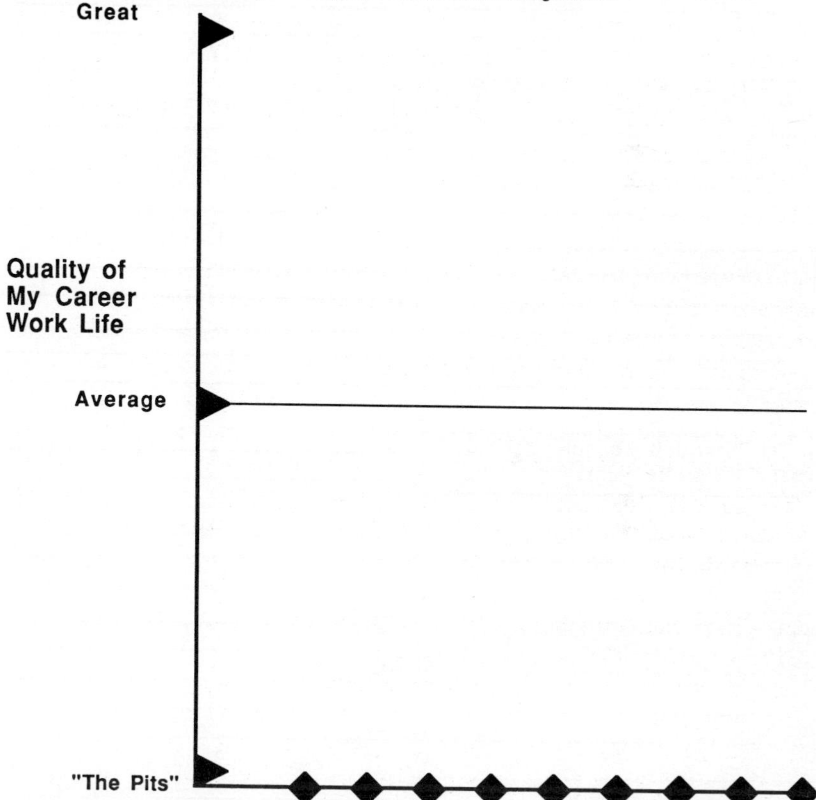

Let each of the marks across the bottom line on this chart represent about five years in your career. If you have worked only a short time, you may let each mark represent a briefer time span. Place a dot for each time interval on the chart that represents how you felt about your career at that point. Connect the dots to form your career life line.

Exhibit 7-4
Sample Self-Assessment

ACCOMPLISHMENTS

A. Childhood through High School

B. College or Special Training

C. First Full-Time Job

D. First Job Change
(or 1-3 years later)

E. Next Job Change
(or 1-3 years later)

F. Next Job Change

G. Current Position

Exhibit 7-5
Sample Self-Assessment
Sorting Out Work Values

One way to better understand self is to identify our values and determine our strength of conviction. Values are those social, moral, and ethical standards that we have acquired over our lifetime. They underlie every decision and course of action. Problems arise when we must make choices that involve conflicting values. At work this could mean making a decision to accept a new position with extensive overtime and travel versus the current position with adequate time for family and civic activities.

Satisfaction at work is frequently determined by the extent to which we can live our values in our job. In selecting a career, career path, or job, it is important to compare the demands and activities of the job with one's values.

Listed below are 36 commonly held values. Select *five* of the items that you value **most**. Mark these with an **M** in the space provided. Then identify *five* items that you value **least**. Mark these with an **L**.

Values List

Decision Making	________	Mental Stimulation	________
Security	________	Knowledge	________
Friendships	________	Creative Expression	________
Independence	________	Fast Pace	________
Work With Others	________	Helping Others	________
Status	________	Challenging Problems	________
Help Society	________	Change and Variety	________
Aesthetics	________	Exercise Competence	________
Work Alone	________	Recognition	________
Stability	________	Affiliation	________
Excitement	________	Public Contact	________
Competition	________	Moral Fulfillment	________
Job Tranquility	________	High Earnings Anticipated	________
Pressure	________	Influence People	________
Work on Frontiers of Knowledge	________	Artistic	________
Location	________	Physical Challenge	________
Time Freedom	________	Precision Work	________
Power and Authority	________	Leadership	________

Understanding what you <u>do</u> and <u>do not</u> value about work will improve your decisions.

Similar to the work skills exercises, inventories of *career management skills* assess the proficiency of the individual in areas of life and career management.

Knowledge inventories are used in career planning workbooks when it is important for individuals to recognize the different disciplines required to function effectively in various parts of the company. Like skills inventories, these generally present a list for the individual to rank or rate.

Through style inventories, lists of individual descriptors, or cases, participants identify those *personality-based aspects* of themselves that are likely to influence successful career choices.

Information about the Organization and Work Options Available

This section of career planning workbooks takes a great deal of time and care to develop. It must include information that is current and specific enough to be of value, without including so much data that it is cumbersome or impossible to manage.

Needs met: This part of the career planning workbook meets the needs employees have to understand the different functional areas within the company, acquire information about what kinds of people fit well in different functions, and examine options that may be available, now or in the future. This is the portion of the book that personalizes career planning for your organization. It provides realistic information and presents career moves that fit with your culture and your business.

Desired results: This section should answer questions about what work exists within the organization, where opportunities exist, what it takes to succeed in different functions within the business, and how to get more specific information about jobs that interest the workbook user. This section may also include more general information about career directions and about the organization's philosophy concerning career movement (geographic moves must be promotions, company encourages lateral moves). The effectiveness of this section can be judged by the degree to which employees are likely to say after completing it, "Now I know where I might fit and why."

Information and exercises frequently included: This portion of the workbook tends to have more information than exercises. Exhibit 7-6 provides a sample of material for this section from an existing career planning workbook.

Typical information about the organization and career options within it are described below.

An organizational overview presents graphically, and perhaps in narrative as well, a "big picture" of the organization, its divisions, branches, products, and services. Sometimes it also describes major directions of the business (expanding overseas, focusing on retail operations) and presents information about growth in different areas of the company.

Exhibit 7-6
Information about Work

Administrative Services

uild-
es into
nt has
ations
assis-
Com-
rocess-
quiring
rrespon-
are pro-
is the de-
f corporate
he develop-
Company.
printed
he Cor-
icating
pplies
e Sta-
ment
nt a
ecord
micro-
f vital
motive
within
Equip-
leet of
ks and
epart-
oping
ning
ment
o pro-

vide cost-effective, reliable services to our customers.

The General Repair Shop is another operation within Support Services which is vital to Company operations. The Shop repairs and maintains electrical equipment such as motors, voltage regulators, circuit breakers and transformers used in power plants and substations. In addition, craftsmen in the Machine and Carpentry Shops fabricate metal and wood products. And when heavy equipment needs to be handled or transported, trained personnel in the Repair Shop's Equipment Section provide their services.

Management Information Systems

Effective and efficient use of the Company's data and information system is the responsibility of the Management Information Systems Organization. This responsibility is shared by three departments: Development, Operations, and Support.

MIS OPERATIONS

The Operations Department provides resources for the processing of information systems throughout the Company. Within this department, corporate data is prepared for use by computer processing. User-requested jobs are scheduled, controlled, and submitted for processing, and output is distributed. Technical support staff are available to solve problems with computer hardware or software. Using the most current computer technology, staff members process information and make sure the Company's computer equipment meets future processing needs.

MIS DEVELOPMENT

This client service department receives all requests for new or modified systems and information processing equipment. MIS Development makes an initial determination on the conceptual approach for the request and coordinates the arrangements for the appropriate in-house and Southern Company Services Information Services personnel to work on the request.

MIS Development provides assistance to the requestor in conducting needs analysis and feasibility studies, requirements definitions, acceptance testing,

ADMINISTRATIVE SERVICES		
	Gen. Svcs.	General Properties Support Services
	Mgmt. Info. Sys.	MIS Operations MIS Development MIS Support
	Human Resour.	Labor Relations Human Resources Dev Personnel
		Risk Management

Reproduced from materials published by Georgia Power Co., Atlanta, Ga.

Major functions within the organization (e.g., finance, manufacturing, information systems) are described to present an idea about the kind of work done and the major skills and knowledge, as well as any special qualities, needed to work in each area.

Workbooks often include a section describing *information interviewing techniques*. The skills important to set up interviews and to manage them effectively are presented. Sample questions may be included to help career planners develop questions that fit their personal needs.

You may want to include information about *career direction options*, other than the traditional vertical movement, to point out the benefits of moving laterally, of growing in place, of expanding or enriching the current job, or of taking on temporary assignments to prepare for future moves. Such information becomes especially meaningful when it is are combined with case studies of individuals who have used each method to reach long-term career goals.

❦ *Goal Setting and Decision Making*

When most people think of career planning, they think of setting goals and making decisions. This section of the workbook is important because it begins to bring into focus the full implications of earlier sections.

Needs met: Of all the sections of a career planning workbook, this is potentially the most important. Without information and exercises to promote goal setting and decision making, the other information in the workbook becomes, at best, interesting and, at worst, useless. This section should be designed to compel career planners to begin making choices and establishing career goals that will motivate them to action.

Desired results: This portion of the career planning workbook will be successful when, after completing it, career planners are able to

1. Describe their long-range (three to five years) goals
2. Identify optional short-range (six months to three years) goals to support their long-range goals
3. Evaluate the consequences of a variety of different career choices

Information and exercises frequently included: Care should be taken in designing this section to ensure that the exercises flow logically, guiding the participant through a sequence of steps toward making some important personal decisions. Most often, information moves from discussions and exercises that promote long-range goal setting to information and exercises designed to increase the individual's effectiveness in establishing short-range goals and making decisions.

One component often included is an exercise that helps career planners think beyond the challenges of today and project themselves into the future. Through a visioning exercise, guided imagery, or open-ended story lines, individuals examine what true satisfaction will be like toward the end of their careers. They take these images and translate them into concrete descriptions of the "milestones" that will mark progress toward these long-term goals.

A second important component consists of information and exercises to help translate broad or vague goal statements into specific, identifiable short-term objectives. Decision-making information and exercises may focus first on decision styles, or on blocks to effective decision making. Those completing the workbook may be asked to identify a variety of decisions they have made and to describe the decision-making process they went through. Then some tips or advice for making better decisions are offered. Here, introducing a decision matrix or balance sheet and describing the need to balance the "data" and the "intuitive" sides of decisions provide new tools and new information for many career planners. The section may conclude with an action plan for completing the process of decision making.

❦ *Resources to Support Employee Career Development*

When included in career planning workbooks, this section builds an effective bridge to other programs, procedures, and people who are important to the organization's career development efforts.

Needs met: The information presented in the resources portion of a career planning workbook helps employees see how their career planning efforts fit with other systems within the organization. It helps them identify additional support for their career planning and gives them backup resources (both publications and people) to keep their career efforts on track.

Desired results: After completing this section, employees should have

1. A clear understanding of who in the organization can help them with career issues
2. A description of other programs, workshops, or procedures that are designed to promote employee career development

Information and exercises frequently included: This section typically includes models, narratives, and other charts showing the people and programs that support employee career development. These may include people in the organization who serve as career advisers, training programs that prepare employees for new opportunities, people in human resources or personnel who have specific career-related responsibilities, guidelines for benefits that support employee education and development, and descriptions of how jobs are filled within the organization.

If career discussions between managers and their employees are part of the career development system of an organization, this process is often described in the resources section. Exercises help the employee think through each of the steps called for in an effective career discussion. Sometimes a career discussion planning guide is included as a tool to help the employee prepare for this discussion. Some workbooks even have sections designed to build skills that help the discussion become more effective. Preparing for the discussion, active listening, responding, negotiating, and developing alternatives are among the skills that may be presented. Exhibit 7-7 shows sample materials from the resources section of an organization's career planning workbook.

❦ *Action Planning and Implementation*

Career planning workbooks most often end with the development of a specific career plan and some form of action or implementation planning exercise. The premise is that even excellent career plans will need some immediate action and reinforcement in order to maintain their momentum.

Needs met: Ending a workbook with action planning and implementation provides the career planner with a clear series of "next steps." Included in this will likely be a written career plan (even if it is a tentative one), unless this plan was developed in the section on goal setting. This career plan is the "product" that is the result of the work done throughout the workbook. Completing it provides a sense of accomplishment and closure. Also included may be a short-range action plan—a source of ongoing energy for continuing the process of career planning and moving toward the goals determined during the goal-setting process.

Desired results: After completing this section of the workbook, employees should have

1. A career plan
2. Specific steps they plan to take to implement their career plans
3. Back-up or contingency plans for moving toward their career goals

Information and exercises frequently included: This section typically consists of forms, documents to provide structure for planning. See Exhibit 7-8 for a sample. Narrative information included here primarily reinforces the importance of taking immediate action to maintain the momentum for career development. Sometimes information on potential obstacles and ways to overcome them are included as well. How to manage your boss, developing skills in organizational politics, and communicating effectively are some likely topics.

Exhibit 7-7
Description of Resources from Organizational Career Development Materials

Chapter 1 introduced a systems perspective of Career Development. Now it is time to look more closely at the resources that can assist you with your personal career planning and development.

CAREER INFORMATION CENTER - These centers, which are currently being piloted and expected to be available in most organizations soon, provide information and resources for career and other self-directed tools for career planning. Called **The Source**, these centers provide easy access to a variety of publication and videotapes and house a wide array of career development materials, from Career Path Guidelines and self-assessments to course bulletins and software packages. The information is designed to help you establish your professional goals and assess the traits and actions necessary to be successful. Among the specific resources found are:

- ✓ Local college and university bulletins
- ✓ Tuition reimbursement forms
- ✓ Books and list of popular books on career planning
- ✓ Self-assessment tests on career aptitudes and interests
- ✓ EDUCATE interactive software to identify courses available through Corporate Education
- ✓ Quarterly and Annual Reports
- ✓ Company publications
- ✓ Company Awareness Program print materials and videotapes

From NCR employee career planning workbook, *Creating Value through Career Planning at NCR*, 1990. Used with permission.

❦ *Variations*

Career planning workbooks vary from glossy, four-color books with professional layout and design to inexpensive photocopied materials bound in notebooks or folders—and to everything in between. In making decisions about the workbook keep these considerations in mind:

Exhibit 7-8
Career Planning Form

1. Personal Profile

1. Myers-Briggs: Type ______

Related Strengths: ________
____
____

2. Strong-Campbell:

Code ____________________

Related Occupations _______
____
____

3. BellSouth Abilities Battery:

Highest Ability Areas ______
____
____
____

4. BellSouth Interest Inventory:

Major Interest Areas ________
____
____

5. Current Areas of Qualification:

Tests you have passed to qualify for company jobs ____
____
____
____

6. Other:

Results of other tests or inventories
____
____
____
____
____
____

Current Career Issues for Me:

Most Important Values	Career Anchors
1. ____________	____________
2. ____________	____________
3. ____________	____________
4. ____________	____________
5. ____________	____________

Career Path Pattern

Skills I Enjoy Using	Interests
____________	____________
____________	____________
____________	____________

My Ideal Career Future

Important Life Goals

Financial Change Goals

Purpose–If the book is to serve as a public relations piece to go to other companies, stockholders, or recruiters, you may find that the extra dollars are well spent in publishing an impressive-looking document. On the other hand, if your company wishes to use the career planning workbook only with employees within the company and especially if the culture of the organization encourages cost savings whenever possible, an expensively published book may not be well received.

Length–If your target group consists of people unaccustomed to working hours for task completion, you might be wise to develop a brief workbook. If the people you hope to have use your career planning workbook are technical and enjoy working with lots of details, a longer book is appropriate.

Content–Even though we have described the typical content for career planning workbooks, you may wish to add or subtract major content areas to fit the learning objectives or the special needs of your audience and your organization.

Distribution–Some workbooks are distributed only in conjunction with other career planning processes (e.g., career counseling or a career planning workshop). Other times, organizations distribute the workbooks to all employees or to all members of certain groups of employees. Most often, regardless of other distribution methods, copies are available in the career center, if you have one.

Balance of Exercises and Information–Some workbooks are as much as 75 percent exercises and discussions of these exercises; others are more than 50 percent narrative. The balance you choose should depend on the purposes of the workbook and on the identified learning styles of your target audience.

Special Features–Variations come from the special features included in a workbook, for example, a career interest form that is a tear-out, self-mail card that employees send in for more specific information about one area of the company. Another variation that adds value to workbooks is a summary section at the conclusion of each chapter, to make sure that readers do not lose sight of where they are going in the midst of the activities designed to get them there. At least one high-tech company has made its workbook available on computer disk. Employees can insert the disk into their personal computers and have a paperless (and easily updated) workbook.

Evaluation Techniques

Evaluating the effectiveness of a career planning workbook should be done in ways that provide the information needed by you and other decision makers. Some of the strategies for evaluation used by organizations publishing workbooks are described here.

Readership One measure of a workbook's effectiveness is the number of employees who choose to use it. If people must exert some effort to obtain a workbook, then one measure of its appeal is the number of people who pick up a copy, send in the form to have a copy sent to them, or take whatever steps are needed to obtain one. Even though this does not measure the impact of the workbook, it is one measure some organizations find useful.

Reaction You may want to include a loose page in the back of the workbook asking those who use it to let you know their reactions. You may construct a checklist of items you want to ask them about (e.g., readability, usefulness of exercises) and leave space for their comments.

Action Sometimes workbooks include something in the last section that requires specific action on the part of users. The number of employees filing a career plan in personnel, sending in a career interest form, or taking some other action requested in the materials is a measure of the effectiveness of the material. You might also be able to qualitatively evaluate some of these actions. If career plans are filed, are they complete? Do they show thoughtfulness and thoroughness? Are they realistic?

Results Following up with employees who use the career planning workbook to see what, if any, results occur from its use can provide you with a wealth of information about which people in which circumstances are likely to get the most benefit from career planning workbooks. This follow-up may be done by tracking moves, auditing career discussion results, interviews, or other methods. In addition to determining the effectiveness of the existing materials, you may also find valuable insights for revising materials based on what people are, and are not, able to do after completing the book.

FOR FURTHER STUDY

There is little specific information available about constructing career planning workbooks. Useful background information may be obtained from examining materials on how to design self-paced learning, including Mager's series on instructional design (1968, 1973, 1975; Mager and Pipe 1970). You may also want to refer to Gutteridge and Otte (1983) to find the resources for developing career planning workshops and an overview of career workbooks. Some of the best background may come from examining published workbooks to see what approaches are used and how the content flows.

CHAPTER 8

❦ ❦

Other Practices andSpecial Populations

The Career Development Task Force is nearing the end of the design phase, and Jim, the chairperson, summarizes. "O.K. See if you agree. We've reached several conclusions. First, the job posting and tuition reimbursement systems we already have could be improved considerably if they were made a part of the total career system. Also, these activities are critical to the system reaching its goal of providing maximum opportunities for employee development in light of organizational goals."

"Second, we want to provide services to employees in remote locations. We'll do this through career planning computer software for use on their personal computers, computerized job posting, and telephone delivered career counseling. Finally, we'll provide for the special needs of women, minorities, high potential managers, and executives."

The task force members nod approvingly. "Good!" says Jim, "We can finish drafting our design proposal. Let's go celebrate."

❦ *Value*

You may ask if job posting and tuition reimbursement are valid components in career development. To us, they are a vital part of a total career system. Job posting that is designed so that appropriate applicants are quickly identified can benefit the organization greatly. When the more complex jobs are filled from inside the company, there is a better guarantee of getting qualified people, and less time is required for "coming up to speed" in new positions.

A major factor in having employees ready to move and to adapt quickly when positions are open is training and development. Individualized employee development is facilitated and enhanced through a tuition reimbursement program. It can also be used for some levels of outplacement by providing reimbursement for off-site career planning workshops for individuals.

Individualized career planning using computer software designed for personal computers may well be on the cutting edge of career development. The potential of this approach is yet to be explored in depth. It offers the possibility for cost-effective, interesting, and highly efficient career assistance when used as part of a total career system.

❦ *Chapter Organization*

In this chapter you will find

1. Definitions of terms used in tuition reimbursement, job posting, computerized career assistance, and adaptations of career development practices for special populations—that is; women, minorities, high potential managers, and executives
2. An overview of tuition reimbursement, job posting, computerized career assistance, and ways of adapting career development practices for special populations
3. A discussion of decisions you will need to make as you design and implement these practices or adaptations
4. Detailed discussions of tuition reimbursement, job posting, computerized career assistance, and ways of adapting career development practices for special populations and how these practices fit into the total career development system
5. Evaluation techniques
6. Resources for further study

❦ *Learning Objectives*

In this chapter you will learn the basics of tuition reimbursement, job posting, computerized career assistance, and ways of adapting career development practices for special populations. After reading this chapter you will be able to

1. Describe these practices and how they fit into a total career development system
2. State the decisions that need to be made to design and implement these practices

3. Locate materials and resources needed
4. Evaluate these components
5. Continue your study in these areas

DEFINITIONS

A number of terms are used in this chapter, perhaps in ways slightly different from what you are accustomed to seeing.

Tuition reimbursement may also be referred to as tuition refund, tuition aid, educational assistance, or tuition advancement (Johnson 1990). Employers either advance or reimburse all or part of the costs for tuition for employee development. *Job posting* is a way of communicating to employees the availability of jobs within the organization. It may be closely linked to a *job bidding* system, in which employees compete for slots based on specified criteria, typically including seniority. *Computerized career development assistance* refers to a range of individualized, computer-delivered services that teach career planning, guide individual assessment, or provide career information. This information may be either internal or external to the organization or both.

High potential managers are those who have been identified by the organization as having the potential to move to executive-level positions. *Executives* fill the top management positions of an organization: chairman of the board, chief executive officer, president, chief financial officer, executive vice president and the like. The focus in this chapter is on somewhat lower positions but clearly on those above middle management. *Women*, as a focus for career development programs, refers to female employees at all levels, but career development programs specifically for women and minorities are typically targeted at middle management positions and below. *Minorities* are all non-white employees.

OVERVIEW

This chapter primarily discusses two practices that can be vital supports to other career development components: tuition reimbursement and job posting. Computerized career assistance and ways in which career development practices can be adapted to fit the special needs of particular special populations—high potential managers, executives, women, and minorities—are also described briefly.

Individualizing to fit special needs is the theme here. Computerized career development assistance potentially can provide all employees with tools for personal career management. They need not have access to counseling, advising, or workshop components, although the total career system is more effective when they do. Tuition reimbursement ideally allows all employees access to development options. They need not always have access to in-house training. Finally, job posting, at its best, allows all employees an opportunity to compete for almost any position in the organization.

What is possible in theory may not be possible in practice. There are constraints, both in the individuals and in the organization. However, with components to provide individualization, and with an attempt to adapt all components to the particular needs of special populations, an effective career development system can be maintained.

Decisions to Make about Individualized Practices

When dealing with ways of individualizing career development practices and of adapting them to the needs of special groups, there are some general questions that need to be addressed. Senior management should be concerned as well, for top-level policies may be involved, either because of a need to be consistent with what is already in place, or in terms of new or revised policies being needed.

What will be the impact on the organization if a group is, or is not, singled out for special consideration? This question is relevant whenever you try to adapt practices to a particular group that you see as having a problem in your organization. Whether or not a problem has been noticed, however, failure to focus attention on special groups may run the risk of serving them poorly. Targeting services for such groups, of course, does risk accusations of favoritism or reverse discrimination. The greater risks appear to us to be associated with failing to attend to special groups, but the probable impact of providing special programs in your unique organizational situation needs to be addressed carefully.

How do we justify special adaptations of services? Either organizational needs or individual needs can justify special attention. Needs met by the various practices discussed below will be outlined for each case.

What special adaptations are needed? To identify needed adaptations, start by recalling three basics. (1) Career development practices, in keeping with other good human resources functions, seek to bring about an optimum match of organizational and individual needs. (2) Individuals need opportunities for development and for using their talents and abilities. (3) Organizations need the best match of people and positions that can be achieved given other needs and constraints. Therefore, if you look for misplaced human resources and for people without the opportunities they need, you'll identify both basic career development system needs and the special adaptations required in order to have the best possible system.

TUITION REIMBURSEMENT

Needs Met: Many organizations, for a variety of reasons, encourage employees to pursue baccalaureate or advanced degree programs. Tuition reimbursement is one way that organizations demonstrate their commitment to education and help make education affordable.

Results Desired: A successful tuition reimbursement component is one that achieves organizational objectives for employee development. Whatever the philosophy behind it, however, employee participation is one measure of its success. Settle (1987) says that typically less than 10 percent of eligible employees are participating at any given time. Relevance of the training and coursework undertaken by employees to the competencies needed in order to achieve business objectives is another indicator of success. Consequently, relevance of any given course of study must be defined in light of employee needs in a particular work organization.

Depending on organizational objectives, success could also include participation by family members in a family educational assistance program or in employee leaves of absence for education.

Brief Narrative of Activities Involved: Creating a good tuition reimbursement program involves a number of steps. The first step is to develop organizational policy and related procedures in this area if they are not already in place. Investigate what other organizations like yours do, conduct a needs assessment on your own, then make a recommendation, and secure the needed approvals.

Bush (1990) recommends asking the following questions when studying practices in other organizations:

- Do you have an educational assistance policy? How does it work?
- Who is eligible to participate in this program?
- To receive assistance, does the employee need to take job-related courses? Does he or she need to be working toward a degree?
- What is your schedule of reimbursement? Do you have a maximum ceiling?

- If an employee wishes to attend a high-tuition university, does your company agree to pay the cost? If not, what alternatives do you offer?
- How do you guarantee a return on your investment in the employee's education?
- Do you have a separate policy for employees chosen by management to participate in a particular academic program, for example, an executive MBA program?
- If class attendance will disrupt the employee's normal working hours, how do you handle that conflict? *

Bush (1990) and Johnson (1990) recommend that your draft policy and procedures document include such things as purpose, scope, application process for each type of educational assistance available, procedures for academic programs for which management chooses the participants, student loans if available, and any special courses or programs that are highly desirable for employees to take.

You may need to do part of steps two and three below as part of your preliminary investigation. Resources listed below may be helpful in this initial work.

The second step is to ensure relevance of college courses and post secondary technical training to organizational and individual objectives. To do this, partnerships must be formed between the work organization and higher education institutions. This concept, along with do's and don'ts has been discussed by Settle (1987).** He suggests personally getting to know the people who can help you in nearby institutions in order to discover matches of interests and values. He recommends a high-level meeting, perhaps the vice president for human resources from your organization with the dean for academic affairs. Informal contacts through social clubs and civic associations should also be pursued.

According to Settle (1987), the third step in creating a viable tuition reimbursement program is to discuss the quality and cost of available and potential offerings. Quality of continuing education programs is likely to be higher if they are closely tied to academic programs. You then are more likely to have access to regular faculty who are committed to forming relationships with the business community. In such situations faculty are more likely to be willing to deliver courses on site and to be more acquainted with adult learners.

Variations Possible: Settle (1987) suggests considering such things as alternate delivery systems. Traditional classrooms may be replaced with tele-

*Bush, Jennifer, 1990, Atlanta, Georgia, personal communication.

**Settle, Theodore J., "Colleges and Universities", in *Training and Development Handbook*, 3 ed, Robert L. Craig, editor, McGraw-Hill, copyright 1987.

vised class sessions or with self-study assignments. Nontraditional institutions, such as the National Technological University, offer both credit and noncredit courses. There are many such nontraditional institutions. Settle also indicates potential promise in working with institutions that give credit for life experience or competency testing. It can take several forms.

Smith (1983) reported a program at Kimberly-Clark that was more broad based than most. It included employee tuition reimbursement linked to self-development plans, family educational assistance tied to employee contributions, and educational leaves of absence.

❦ *Helpful Resources*

If you need an overview of common practices, perhaps as a basis for justifying being either traditional or innovative in your own organization, resources are available through the Society for Human Resource Management, 606 N. Washington Street, Alexandria, Virginia 22314.

Settle (1987) provides a bibliography that looks helpful, and two other publications that seem highly relevant for further study are the following:

Fenwick, Dorothy D., ed., *Campus-Business Linkage Programs: Education and Business Prospering Together*, 2nd ed. American Council on Education/Macmillan Series in Higher Education. New York: Macmillan, 1986.

Gold, Gerald G., ed., *Business and Higher Education: Toward New Alliances.* New Directions in Experiential Learning, Number 13. San Francisco: Jossey-Bass, 1981.

To see how tuition reimbursement can fit into a total career, training, and/or human resources system, you may want to examine some case studies and related articles such as the following:

DuBois, Carolyn, "Back to School," *The Magazine for Chief Financial Officers*, 3, 11 (November 1987), 86–87, 91.

Gerber, Beverly, "Training at L. L. Bean," *Training* (October 1988), 85–89.

Osborne, Jayne E., How to Find and Retain Staff," *Supervisory Management*, 34, 9 (September), 26–28.

Raudsepp, Eugene, "How Engineers Get Ahead and Avoid Obsolescence," *Machine Design*, 61, 1 (January 1989), 107–111.

Ryland, Elisabeth K., and Benson Rosen, "Attracting Job Applicants with Flexible Benefits," *Personnel*, 65, 3 (March 1988), 71–73.

Sweeney, Dennis C., Jr., Dean Haller, Jr., and Frederick Sale, Jr., "Individually Controlled Career Counseling," *Training and Development Journal* (August 1987), 58–61.

Trunick, Perry A, "Leadership and People Distinguish Federal Express," *Transportation and Distribution*, 30, 13 (December 1989), 18–22.

Wagel, William H., "Hardee's: One Step Ahead in the Race for Employees," *Personnel*, 66, 4 (April 1989), 20–24.

You may need to become informed about tax regulations related to employee benefits. Talking with people in your organization who work regularly in the field is the easiest way to get information. You may also want to consult such journals as *Compensation & Benefits Management.* One example of a helpful article is the following:

Birmingham, Richard J., "Overview of Section 89 Regulations, *Compensation & Benefits Management*, 5, 4 (Summer 1989), 327–331.

JOB POSTING

Job posting may not be the first thing that comes to mind when one thinks about employee career development. Yet, a survey of HRD practices among Fortune 500 companies reported that it was the most often used method (Ralphs and Stephan 1986).

Needs Met: Communicating to employees open positions in the organization can meet both organizational and employee needs. Osborne (1988, 1989) sees job posting as one way of reducing turnover among talented employees. Others see it as a critical component of effective staffing—finding the best people when there are jobs to fill (Stumpf 1988; Mondy, Noe, and Edwards 1987). Organizations also benefit from job posting through such things as good communications, being perceived as fair, lower hiring costs, better use of the work force, and equal opportunity liability reduction—all of which are possible according to survey results presented by Levine (1984).

The same survey also identified employee benefits. They include knowledge of available positions and improved morale that probably results from people finding better matches with positions and coming to believe that their skills are used. Employees who want to avoid becoming overly specialized in a technical position can move laterally, in some organizations, and broaden their experience by using information provided by job posting.

Results Desired: Success in job posting includes meeting organizational and individual needs. The organization needs to have the right people available for job openings as they appear. Employees need opportunities to move within the system to use better their emerging abilities and interests. Success also includes avoiding problems that can make the job posting system unworkable. Following the suggestions outlined in the next section will help to achieve these results.

Brief Narrative of Activities Involved: Writers on the topic agree that a job posting system is most likely to work if it is specifically designed to meet organizational needs and to support an explicit human resources philosophy of promoting from within. This point has been made in early reports of job posting programs such as those at Miles Laboratories (Cummins 1983) and at Augat (Wallrapp 1981), as well as in surveys such as those of *Personnel* readers reported by Rendero (1980) and of *Personnel* readers and human resource managers reported by Levine (1984). These sources and the later works mentioned earlier suggest a number of steps in planning and implementing a job posting system.

1. Do research. Review literature and conduct telephone interviews with people who operate programs in similar organizations. Become familiar with the latest policies, procedures, and problems.

2. Get top level commitment. The CEO needs to agree to support a policy of promoting from within and to review the procedures when they are fully designed. The CEO should be committed to making a public announcement to begin the program.

3. Form a design team. Carefully think through every procedure that is needed. Use a representative mix of human resource staff, line managers, and employees. The design process may take as long as 18 months if you have complex issues and if controversy pervades discussions.

4. Decide who is eligible to apply for positions and who is not. Consider such things as time with the organization and time in present job, level of employment, type of position, geographical location, how many times a year a person may apply, how many applications may be made simultaneously, standing in the organization (e.g., not on probation, performing satisfactorily in current job), and other such factors relevant to your specific situation.

5. Decide what types of positions will be posted and what types will not. Consider whether to post openings created by extensive unit reorganizations, openings occurring from injuries, other such special case positions, entry level, temporary, and part-time positions. Deciding which jobs are posted requires that you examine the benefits and risks associated with posting only certain jobs, as opposed to the benefits and risks for posting all (or, more realistically, all nonexecutive) jobs.

6. Develop standard procedures. You need consistent ways of initiating the announcement of an opening, standardizing the content of the job notice, receiving and screening applications, conducting interviews, notifying the supervisor that an employee is being considered and/or accepted for the position, notifying rejected employees of the decision, and providing feedback and counseling to employees who were not selected.

7. Decide details for the method of posting. Determine when, where, and how the actual posting will be done. Decide what information will be made public with the job posting. If you publish less information, you run the risk of having many unsuitable candidates apply for the job. At the minimum, post with the job opening the required skills, knowledge, and experience. Some organizations post job levels or salary ranges as well.

Announcements should appear at stated times and remain posted for a few days to a week. Consider announcing openings through bulletin boards in lounges or hallways near elevators, regular publications, handouts, meetings, and direct mail if there is not a way to computerize the system in a user-friendly way.

8. Decide what feedback will be given to those who apply. In some cases, all applicants are given specific information about how their qualifications matched, or did not match, with those of the job. Other times, only those applicants who actually are interviewed for the opening receive feedback. This issue is a delicate one. Your answer will depend on the culture of the organization, the resources available to provide feedback, and your organization's philosophy about openness of information.

9. Decide how long to delay external searches. You need to delay long enough to give ample opportunity for internal applicants to state their intentions. On the other hand, creating staffing problems is undesirable. A week may be about enough.

10. Decide how the job posting system will be administered. The range of options here extends from a paper-and-pencil system, in which applicants fill out applications (for consideration by internal staffing specialists and managers) to computerized systems in which applicants key in information for a data bank (to be examined by those who will make the decisions about whom to interview or hire). When designing forms, focus on the function of the forms. Ask yourself what decisions will be made by the people using them and what data are needed for those decisions. Work toward keeping the forms simple and eliminating all the "nice to know" information.

11. Determine guidelines for transfers. Supervisors need notice that an employee will be leaving and transferring to a new position. Adequate notice prevents problems that an abrupt loss of the person might cause.

12. Determine recognition and follow-up procedures. When employees are promoted as a result of the system, consider putting names in publications and/or on bulletin boards. It is important to communicate that the system works. Individual recognition gets attention.

13. Avoid "bad luck"; anticipate and avoid problems. Successful job posting also involves operating the system so as to avoid problems such as those identified by Levine (1984). They include the following:

- Unqualified applicants may post for positions and make selection burdensome.
- Employees may form perceptions of outcomes being "rigged,"—of the job posting system being a sham.
- Filling one opening may cause a chain reaction as each position filled internally creates another opening.
- Employees who post repeatedly and are turned down each time may become very discouraged and dissatisfied.

These difficulties cannot be avoided altogether. They are minimized, however, with job posting systems that have clearly communicated procedures, full information about the vacant position, and consistency with other career development processes.

***Clearly communicated procedures*:** When everyone knows what to expect, problems are minimized. When these procedures expedite the selection process and limit perceived "game playing," they add credibility to the posting process. For example, one company, wanting to avoid having employees see the system as a sham, allowed certain jobs with a readily available successor within the same department to bypass the posting process. Another organization whose goal was to open up the number of applicants beyond the more obvious candidates within the department required a certain number of candidates to be interviewed from outside the department before the job could be filled, assuming that candidates were identified through job posting. Regardless of the guidelines you adopt, they should be widely communicated and consistently followed.

***Full information about the vacant position*:** The more information employees have about a position, the more likely they will be to post for jobs that are appropriate to them. Whether or not to make public salary ranges and other sensitive information must be decided by your organization. Remember, however, that the trade-off for limited information is less data for employees to use and the increased likelihood that people will post for jobs that are inappropriate for them.

***Consistency with other career development processes*:** When job posting is considered an integral part of the organization's career development system and links with other components, it is more likely to be successful. For example, if employees are introduced to job posting in a career workshop or if they go to the career resource center to post for jobs, they can be given information about how to use the posting system most effectively. If those employees who post often or who post for jobs that seem to be poor fits with their skills and experience are referred to a career adviser or counselor, they may learn strategies to help them accomplish their career goals and avoid the frustrations of fruitless posting. One organization even proposed that employees could only post for jobs that were consistent with their career development plans on file in the personnel department.

Also, techniques can be developed for avoiding such things as reality shock—the traumatic surprise and rude awakening that come with employees' discovering that the job is not at all what they had in mind. Allowing a "tryout" in the new position for a few days is one possibility.

❦ *Helpful Resources*

As with some other practices, other people may be the best resource in learning about job posting for particular types of organizations. The practice seems to differ by type of organization. Networking through professional organizations, such as the Career Development Professional Practice Area of the American Society for Training and Development (ASTD) or the Society for Human Resource Management (SHRM), is probably a good place to start.

Computerized Career Assistance

Other useful tools in the implementation of a complete career development system include computerized approaches to career assessment, goal setting, and providing information about work. Technological advances have made numerous career hardware and software components available that individualize or speed up such things for human resources personnel. We have chosen to describe a few very different packages, just to give you an idea of the diverse possibilities available.

DISCOVER for Organizations

DISCOVER for Organizations software, available from the American College Testing Program (ACT), is a computer-based career management system for employees. DISCOVER operates on an IBM personal computer with 256K RAM, 10 megabytes of storage and a color monitor (or compatible hardware). No previous computer experience is necessary to use it.

The career management approach that is used involves four steps. Each of the four sections can be used independently. Employees may (1) learn about themselves—interests, skills, and work-related values and preferences—and usefully organize that information; (2) learn about their organization to determine which career opportunities best fit their interests and skills; (3) identify available career options and formulate a plan of action to move in one of those directions; and/or (4) find assistance in implementing action plans through accessing detailed information on training and education opportunities, networking and job interviewing skills, and résumé and cover letter writing. Within each of these steps there are options.

Support services are available. Among other things, they include a guide for professional staff—the Human Resource Development Manual, a guide for employees—the User's Guide, and a paper-and-pencil version of the assessment exercises—the Career Management Guidebooks.

DISCOVER for Organizations can be used as a stand-alone system, although professional career counseling support is desirable. It may also be a component of one-to-one counseling or of a career seminar. It can be customized in a number of ways, has a built in evaluation feature, and can produce reports on employee evaluations of the system or employee demographic data.

Because DISCOVER is a complete, self-contained career management system, HR staff need not be directly involved in many of its uses, although employees may need help in interpreting and applying the results. This software also keeps records on its use for accountability and research purposes.

For more information and for a demonstration version of DISCOVER, contact ACT at 319-337-1000, or write to The American College Testing Program, Discover Services,, 2201 North Dodge, P.O. Box 168, Iowa City, Iowa 52243.

The Placement Problem Solver

At times, organizations may want to include an internal outplacement service as a career development component—perhaps through a career center. The Placement Problem Solver (PPS) by CAPCO: The Capability Corporation generates complete vocational reports for planning and placement.

PPS identifies occupations based on transferable skills, interests, or industrial experience. PPS reports provide national and statewide labor force statistics (all 50 states), estimates of national or local wages (more then 2,800 U.S cities), information about schools, and lists of businesses (name, address, phone) to encourage job search for outplacement or employee/spouse relocation. CAPCO maintains information on more than 8 million businesses throughout the United States. The business listings (which are also useful for labor market survey) can be selected by zip code(s), county (or multiple counties), and minimum number of employees.

Because the CAPCO data base is too large for typical microcomputers (more than three billion bytes of data), users access the CAPCO computer by a (usually) local phone call through modem dial-up using an existing microcomputer or terminal. Users may also lease a system from CAPCO or have CAPCO custom-design a system for use on company computing equipment. Use of the PPS is available on a per case, per service, per connect time, or flat-rate basis. For HR personnel who do not have access to computer equipment, CAPCO also has economical prepaid forms available. Just complete the prepaid form (no expiration date), mail or fax it to CAPCO, and CAPCO processes and mails the report. Phone-in service is also available.

HR personnel can use the PPS to look up occupational information by Dictionary of Occupational Titles code, job title, or partial title to identify alternate occupations by means of an employee's transferable skills, interests, and experience or to survey the labor market for comparative wage and skill information. The PPS has a built-in job bank for storing current company vacancies and for matching vacancies to available employees or new applicants The job bank can also be used to house information about all job positions within a company, which can be searched to find suitable light-duty work for injured employees who seek early return-to-work opportunities. PPS can also be used for post-injury analysis of employees, for corporate outplacement, and vocational rehabilitation placements. CAPCO has a special program for worker compensation and other liability issues called Pre-Injury/Post-Injury Analysis

(PREPOST) It determines occupational loss and changes in wages for those lost occupations.

CAPCO products are user friendly. CAPCO provides HR personnel with toll-free support. For more information on PPS or PREPOST, contact CAPCO at East 5805 Sharp, Suite 103, Spokane, Washington, 99212 or call 1-800-541-5006.

❦ *Micro-Q*

Personnel Decisions, Inc. (PDI) has developed a family of job analysis tools called HR FOCUS, one component of which is Micro-Q, a PC-based software system. Micro-Q software enables HR personnel to store and process job analysis data—job descriptions, compensation information, job component values, career pathing information, and performance appraisal criteria— all in a standard, easily accessed format. The data editing feature of the software permits quick updating of job descriptions or component values as the work environment changes.

In order to compile accurate job descriptions and component values, company employees complete either standard or custom-designed job analysis questionnaires; the questionnaires are then processed using Micro-Q to generate individual and group job descriptions/job evaluations. HR personnel can also use the Micro-Q data base to assess training and development needs.

Two optional Micro-Q modules are available. First, the performance appraisal system can generate customized performance appraisal forms directly from the job information data base. Forms can include such information as job objectives, time spent on duties and tasks, job component effectiveness ratings, overall job ratings, major responsibility summaries, performance against goals, and development plans. Second, a career pathing module can provide graphic reports, showing the similarities and differences between existing job and future job characteristics.

Micro-Q is available on a site-license basis or on a service-by-PDI basis. To be used on site, Micro-Q requires an IBM PC/386 or compatible hardware with 640KB RAM, a 20 MB fixed disk or larger, an HP LaserJetII or compatible printer, and MS- DOS 2.1 or above. User-friendly directions make exploration of career options possible for those with minimal computer experience, and a customer hotline for help is available.

For more information about Micro-Q, contact Seymour Uranowitz or Dwain Boelter at Personnel Decisions, Inc., 2000 Plaza VII Tower, 45 South Seventh Street, Minneapolis, Minnesota 55402, or call 612-339-0927.

❦ *Other Applications*

In some organizations, computer data bases have been created with computer programs that allow employees to browse through a directory of positions that exist throughout the organization. Information on qualifications needed for each job as well as on the demands of the job are presented.

Human Resource Information Systems (HRIS) often include career planning and development data. A system may allow human resource specialists or managers to initiate searches to identify employees with specific skills, experience, or interests. Some advanced versions allow employees to search for jobs with characteristics most like their personal preferences. Though few truly integrated systems currently exist, the use of computerized information to support other career development components is one of the important innovative practices in career development.

One very specific application is the scoring of inventories such as the *Strong-Campbell Interest Inventory (SCII)*. Joan Massola (1990) of the Pacific Bell Employee Career Center in San Ramon, California, indicated that they purchased software and other equipment needed for scoring the SCII from Consulting Psychologists Press. It enables them to report results of the SCII in minutes if needed. Massola reports that it works well but that you should pay careful attention to the scanner you purchase. She suggests that you must anticipate the scoring of at least 500 inventories for the system to be cost-effective. If you have considerably more than 500, you can really benefit from reduced costs.

❦ *Helpful Resources*

Probably the most helpful resource in this area is other people, for several reasons. Technology changes fast. Systems have peculiarities that are not emphasized in the literature. Networking in professional organizations is a good place to start. Make contact with people in the Career Development Practice Area of the American Society for Training and Development, the Society for Human Resource Management, and the Career Development Division of the American Association for Counseling and Development. People in other fields who may have valuable information include rehabilitation counselors, university career planning and placement personnel, and coordinators of career centers.

ADAPTING PRACTICES FOR SPECIAL POPULATIONS

Career development practices must be adapted for special populations—minorities (all nonwhites), women, high potential managers, and high potential executives. Otherwise, the real career issues of these groups will go unaddressed, and their special needs will be unmet.

An understanding of cultural differences is important when planning the adaptation of career development practices. By cultural differences, we mean such things as verbal and nonverbal communication patterns, assumptions that are made about symbolic meanings, behavior norms, perceptions or interpretations of events and behaviors, and expectations. These differences involve values and fundamental belief systems. Different cultures are involved when dealing with various minority groups from different backgrounds, with women, and with top executives. The principles regarding differences that need to be understood are similar for all of these groups (Willis 1990).

We can offer some examples of the need for adapting practices and some processes that may help you to understand what is needed. The issue is too complex, however, for simple rules or standard adaptations. A basic assumption that we are making is that both minorities and women interact with organizational cultures that are dominated by white male ways of thinking and behaving. Schaef (1981) made this point well regarding women's issues a decade or more ago. Career development practices can assist special populations to develop themselves to their fullest—to their own benefit as well as that of the work organization—if their special problems are understood and addressed.

Developing this understanding requires direct, sensitive, unhurried, personal contact by managers and human resource development specialists in order to allow employees to articulate their problems and perspectives. In one case, the president of a very large corporation began having brown bag lunches with two minority groups. After gaining an understanding of their particular needs, he employed a career development coordinator for each group and charged them with developing special programming. This case represents how far it is possible to go when management sees the potential benefits to the organization. It also provides an example of one way of making contact.

Some organizations have human resource training programs to help their managers understand and manage diversity in the workplace. These programs can be extremely helpful for promoting positive relationships between managers and employees whose cultures (including belief systems) are different from their own. Such programs also offer opportunities to foster a "career development perspective" toward nontraditional employees.

❦ *Minorities*

The percentage of nonwhites and first generation Americans in the workplace is increasing. Verna Willis (1990), a person with extensive experience in business and in international consulting, has outlined some of the dimensions to consider. Minorities and people from other countries may bring with them different communication styles. For example, some may appear too aggressive, others too passive; they may be less direct than needed in some situations. Some will stand too close when talking, others too far away. Talking to the "top person" may have great symbolic meaning. Such differences can impact on how they themselves are perceived by their managers, and these differences—if they exist among people in your organization— should be addressed in career planning workshops and in managers' role workshops. Managers must learn to accept, with limits, these differences in order to elicit the energy and creativity of these employees.

Lifestyle expectations may also differ (Willis 1990). For example, they may expect a different work pace. Being "late to work" may have a different meaning; a half hour past the start of the workday may not be considered "late." In the office, "talking instead of working" may be more expected than in the typical American organization. Other expectations may center around time off for family events that the larger society does not consider important enough to warrant leaving work. Such differing expectations need to be brought to the attention of everyone who is likely to be affected so that mutually acceptable accommodations can be made. Again, the training in workshops should be adapted to address these issues.

The very concept of planning, as presented in this book, may itself be foreign (Willis 1990). Some minorities may come from a background in which belief in fate is strong. To these people planning is at best seen as useless. Others will lack skill in making specific commitments such as setting up checklists with deadlines. Some cultures are more oriented to talking and telling within a context of evolving activities than to documenting firm plans on paper. Workshops and career counseling or advising may need to emphasize that plans are flexible, that putting things on paper is part of capturing a vision that can inspire and direct behavior. This vision and related action steps need not assume that one believes that he or she can control the future.

In some cultures, people challenge personal and social intentions and actions rather than the propositions or ideas that have been put forward (Willis 1990). These people are less analytical, less focused on the content of proposals, more likely to look at the personal impact on themselves and their friends, and then to react to that. In some cases this tendency results in a type of consensus that is an agreement to work toward specific goals for the mutual benefit of all concerned, whether or not there is agreement on the principles involved. Career development practices can emphasize individual and organizational benefits to gain commitment in these cases.

❦ *Women*

Women experience different treatment from what men get in the workplace, and they face additional problems. These facts have been outlined well in such books as *Games Mother Never Taught You* (Harragan 1989), *The Organization Woman* (Highman, 1985), and *Altered Ambitions* (Jaffe 1991). Examples over a period of years by one human resources professional (Bush 1990) include such things as being paid less than their male counterparts for doing the same work, being assigned the same work without equivalent titles and office arrangements, and not being considered for senior management positions. Even though some organizations have made some visible efforts to develop women in the professional and managerial ranks, there is little evidence that barriers preventing women's access to executive positions have come down.

To these external organizational barriers to career success we must add the internal barriers within the women themselves, who are not always able to visualize themselves in top leadership roles or who don't know the rules of competition modeled on team sports. Social barriers such as being expected to be full-time careerists and full-time mothers simultaneously also create a different experience for women. A response from Joyce Brothers (1988) was the book *The Successful Woman: How to Have a Career, a Husband, and a Family—And Not Feel Guilty about It.*

Career development practices can be adapted to ensure that gender issues are addressed by providing opportunities for women to clarify their unique concerns and circumstances, and then to brainstorm strategies for achieving personal career objectives. Leaders of career development programs also may get the attention of senior management and advocate for human resource policies and practices that encourage women to plan for career success.

High Potential Managers

People with high potential are also a type of minority group with their own special problems. They face the stress caused by high ambitions and high expectations from the organization. Some organizations set up special career paths for high potential managers, those who have been identified as having unusually great potential and who can move rapidly into senior management positions. Managers in this group face unique problems such as having to win the respect of older employees, overcoming the resentment of their peers who are not on the fast track, and continually living up to high expectations.

The stress generated by their role in the organization suggests several possible adaptations of career development programs. Career counseling may be prescribed by the organization on a regular basis instead of their having to request it. Special information on management careers in the organization can be assembled and delivered to the manager instead of simply letting him or her know that a career center exists. A heavier dose of personality testing also can be prescribed both to assist high potential people in understanding how they fit into work groups best and to assist the organization in planning their movement through various work assignments.

Mentors who can coach and advise high potential managers may be identified and assigned for a period of time. This resource gives the young manager access to a senior person on a regular basis to discuss business or personal concerns.

❦ *High Potential Executives*

Above high potential managers are high potential executives, in the upper ranks of the organization. They are being considered for the very top positions. These executives, too, have concerns about their development, growth, and special career issues. Like the others, this group can also benefit from career development programs. Otte and Cully (1984) report what one organization did for high potential executives. First there were consultations with their managers and with them. Then customized, individual career plans were prepared for them. Plans included self-initiated activities as well as reading and training programs that represented substantial organizational investment. Next, these plans were discussed with their managers and with them. Clarifications and modifications were made as needed. Commitments to the plans were requested of both the high potential executives and of their managers. In short, the organization initiated individualized career development programs for them, fully expecting them to commit to the plans for two reasons. They had opportunity for input, and they were expected to understand that their position made the request for the commitment reasonable.

EVALUATION TECHNIQUES

Anthropological research methods may offer the best guidelines for planning evaluation of career development adaptations for special groups. Using participant observers in the organization is one promising technique. These observers could be employees who are willing to assist the career development staff as part of a task force or other ad hoc group. They should be trained to understand the broad goal of career development programming—obtaining an optimal match of individual and organizational needs. They also need to understand the objectives of the different practices presented in this book. This knowledge will allow them to make judgments regarding whether or not the goals and objectives of career development activities are being achieved for special groups. They also need training in techniques for data collection that involve listening and observing skills.

These observers can then gather data both for needs assessment and for evaluating the effectiveness of career development programs. The data will be qualitative—themes from conversations with members of special groups, observations of nonverbal behavior, case study reports, and other "soft" data. The observers should operate openly, letting people know that they are working on the task force, offering to pass along suggestions.

FOR FURTHER STUDY

To learn more about adapting career development programs in light of cultural diversity, there seems to be no substitute for conducting informal focus groups, such as brown bag lunches, to learn firsthand from employees about their unique issues, circumstances, perceptions, beliefs, values, norms, and expectations. Such groups can become informal advisory committees through their reactions to proposed adaptations of career development programs in response to their needs.

Networking with other career development professionals with similar situations is also highly recommended. Assistance may be found in such professional groups as the American Society for Training and Development.

For a highly readable overview of female/male differences in a mythic, global, historical perspective examine *The Chalice & the Blade* by Riane Eisler (New York: Harper and Row, 1988). Within that perspective it is interesting to study *Women's Reality* by Anne Wilson Schaef (Minneapolis: Winston Press, 1981) and the more current *The Career Psychology of Women* by Nancy E. Betz and Louise F. Fitzgerald (San Diego: Academic Press, 1987).

For developing an understanding of professional women's issues, we recommend *Altered Ambitions* by Betsy Jaffe (1991). Dr. Jaffe is a New York–based, innovative career counselor who works with male and female clients. She was with Catalyst, which promotes careers of executive women, for several years. *Altered Ambitions* provides case histories of five professional women navigating a series of career/life changes. The cases provide a basis for understanding the application of insights from the author's synthesis of new theories and research. *Altered Ambitions* updates *Passages*, *Season's of a Man's Life*, and *Managerial Woman.* Self-directed exercises are built on this foundation for individuals facing changes whether in career, relationships, health, lifestyle, or any combination of these areas.

To understand ways of working with high potential managers, study *The Identification and Development of High Potential Managers* (Executive Knowledge Works, 1987).

❦ ❦

References

CHAPTER 1

McLagan, Patricia, *Models for Excellence.* Alexandria, Va.: American Society for Training and Development, 1989.

CHAPTER 2

Cetron, Marvin, ed., *Careers Tomorrow*, Washington, D.C.: World Future Society, 1988.

Donald, K., and J. Carlysle, "The Diverse Decision-Makers: Helping Students with Career Decisions," *Vocational Guidance Quarterly* (June, 1983).

Driver, Michael, "Career Concepts and Career Management in Organizations," *Behavioral Problems in Organizations* (Gary Cooper, ed.). Englewood Cliffs, N.J.: Prentice Hall, 1979.

Gutteridge, Thomas G., and Fred L. Otte, *Organizational Career Development: State of the Practice.*, Alexandria, Va.: American Society for Training and Development, 1983.

Janis, I., and Dan Wheeler, "Thinking Clearly About Career Choices," *Psychology Today*, May 1978.

Kaye, Beverly L., *Up Is Not the Only Way.* Englewood Cliffs, N.J.: Prentice Hall, 1982.

Slavenski, Lynn and Marilyn Buckner, *Career Development Programs in the Workplace.* Columbus, Ohio: ERIC Clearinghouse on Adult, Career, and Vocational Education, The Center on Education and Training for Employment, The Ohio State University, 1988.

CHAPTER 3

Gutteridge, Thomas G., and Fred L. Otte, *Organizational Career Development: State of the Practice.* Alexandria, Va.: American Society for Training and Development, 1983.

Jones, P. R., B. Kaye, and H. R. Tayler, "You Want Me to Do What?" *Training and Development Journal*, 35, 7 (July 1981), 56–62.

Leibowitz, Zandy, Caela Farren, and Beverly Kaye, *Designing Career Development Systems.* San Francisco: Jossey-Bass, 1986.

Leibowitz, Zandy, and Nancy Schlossberg, "Training Managers for Their Role in a Career Development System," *Training and Development Journal*, 35, 7 (July 1981), 72–79.

Meckel, Nelson T., "The Manager as Counselor," *Training and Development Journal*, 35, 7 (July 1981), 65–69.

Otte, Fred, and Peggy Hutcheson, *Career Development: A Shared Responsibility* (The Manager's Role). Atlanta: Atlanta Resources, Inc. 1985.

Slavenski, Lynn, and Marilyn Buckner, *Career Development Programs in the Workplace.* Columbus, Ohio: ERIC Clearinghouse on Adult, Career, and Vocational Education, The Center on Education and Training for Employment, The Ohio State University, 1988.

Storey, Walter D., *Career Dimensions III.* Croton-on-Hudson, N.Y.: General Electric Co., 1976.

CHAPTER 4

Carkhuff, Robert, *The Skills of Helping: An Introduction to Counseling.* Amherst, Mass.: Human Resource Development Press, 1979.

Crites, John O., *Career Counseling: Models, Methods, and Materials.* New York: McGraw-Hill, 1981.

Egan, Gerard, *The Skilled Helper*, 4th ed. Monterey, Calif.: Brooks/Cole, 1990.

Gutteridge, Thomas G., and Fred L. Otte, *Organizational Career Development: State of the Practice.* Alexandria, Va.: American Society for Training and Development, 1983.

Kapes, Jerome T., and Marjorie M. Mastie, *A Counselor's Guide to Career Assessment Instruments.* Alexandria, Va.: American Association for Counseling and Development, 1988.

The Ninth Mental Measurements Yearbook, vols. I and II, James V. Mitchell, Jr., ed. Lincoln, Nebr.: Boros Institute of Mental Measurements, 1985.

Tests in Print III, James V. Mitchell, Jr., ed. Lincoln, Nebr.: Boros Institute of Mental Measurements, 1983.

Patterson, Cecil H., "Counseling: Self-Clarification and the Helping Relationship," in H. Borow, ed., *Man in a World at Work.* Boston: Houghton Mifflin, 1964, pp. 434–459.

Rogers, Carl., *Counseling and Psychotherapy.* Boston: Houghton Mifflin, 1942.

———,*On Becoming a Person.* Boston: Houghton Mifflin, 1961.

CHAPTER 5

Gutteridge, Thomas G., and Fred L. Otte, *Career Development: State of the Practice.* Alexandria, Va: American Society for Training and Development, 1983.

Marlowe, Anne, Personal communication, 1985.

Otte, Fred L., and Fred R. Cully, "Career Planning for High Potential Upper Level Managers," *Training and Development Journal*, 38, 4 (1984), 81–84.

CHAPTER 6

Amico, A., "Computerized Career Information," *Personnel Journal*, 60, 8 (1981) 632–633.

Bolles, Richard N., *What Color Is Your Parachute?* Berkeley, Calif.: Ten Speed Press, 1990.

Figler, Howard, *The Complete Job-Search Handbook*, rev. and exp. ed. New York: Henry Holt, 1988.

Hubbard, Marlis, and Susan Hawke, *Developing a Career Information Centre*, 2nd rev. ed.. Montreal: Career Information Resource Advisory Group, 1987.

Moir, Elizabeth, "Career Resource Centers in Business and Industry," *Training and Development Journal*, 35, 2 (February 1981).

Stahl, L., " Micros Help Choose Careers," *Computing Canada*, 9, 16, 1983.

CHAPTER 7

Dalton, Gene W., and Paul H. Thompson, *Novations: Strategies for Career Management.* Glenview, Ill.: Scott Foresman, 1986.

Driver, Michael, "Career Concepts and Career Management in Organizations," in Gary Cooper, ed., *Behavioral Problems in Organizations.* Englewood Cliffs, N.J.: Prentice Hall, 1979.

Gutteridge, Thomas G., and Fred Otte, *Career Development: State of the Practice.* Alexandria, Va.: American Society for Training and Development, 1983.

Mager, Robert, *Developing Attitudes Toward Instruction.* Palo Alto, Calif.: Fearon, 1968.

———,*Goal Analysis.* Belmont, Calif.: Fearon, 1973.

———,*Preparing Instructional Objectives.* Belmont, Calif.:
Fearon, 1975.

———,and Peter Pipe, *Analyzing Performance Problems.* Belmont, Calif.: Fearon, 1970.

Super, Donald, *Career Education and the Meaning of Work.* New York: Teachers College, Columbia University, 1975.

CHAPTER 8

Bush, Jennifer, Personal communication, Atlanta, Ga., 1990.

Cummins, Robert B., "Miles Laboratories, Inc. Creates a Job Posting Program," *Personnel Administrator*, 28, 6 (1983), 41–45.

Executive Knowledge Works, *The Identification and Development of High Potential Managers*. Palatine, Ill.: Anthony J. Fresina and Associates, 1987.

Highman, Edith L., *The Organization Woman*. New York: Human Sciences Press, 1985.

Jaffe, Betsy, *Altered Ambitions*. New York: Donald I. Fine, Inc., 1991.

Johnson, Susan G., "Tuition Reimbursement," paper, 1990.

Levine, Hermine Z., "Job Posting Practices," *Personnel*, 61, 6 (November/December 1984), 48–52.

Massola, Joan, Personal communication, 1990.

Mondy, R. Wayne, Robert M. Noe, and Robert E. Edwards, "Successful Recruitment: Matching Sources and Methods," *Personnel*, 64, 9 (September 1987), 42–46.

Osborne, Jayne E., "Rounding Up Your Recruits," *Management World*, 17, 6 (November/December 1988), 7–9.

———,"How to Find and Retain Staff," *Supervisory Management*, 34, 9 (September 1989), 26–28.

Otte, Fred L., and Fred R. Cully, "Career Planning for High-Potential Upper Level Managers," *Training and Development Journal*, 4, 4 (1984) 46–50.

Ralphs, Lenny T., and Eric Stephan, "HRD in the Fortune 500," *Training and Development Journal*, 40, 10 (October 1986), 69–76.

Rendero, Thomasine, "Job-Posting Practices," *Personnel*, 57, 5 (1980), 4–13.

Schaef, Anne Wilson, *Women's Reality*. Minneapolis, Minn.: Winston Press, 1981.

Settle, Theodore J., "Colleges and Universities," in *Training and Development Handbook*, 3rd ed., ed. R. L. Craig. New York: McGraw-Hill, 1987.

Smith, G. B., "Employee-Sponsored Programs," in *Financing Recurring Education*, H. M. Levin and H. G. Schutze, eds. Beverly Hills, Calif.: Sage, 159–187.

Stumpf, Stephen A., "Choosing Career Management Practices to Support Your Business Strategy," *Human Resource Planning*, 11, 1 (1988), 33–47.

Wallrapp, Gary G., " Job Posting for Nonexempt Employees: A Sample Program," *Personnel Journal*, 60, 10 (1981), 796–798.

Willis, Verna J., Personal communication, 1990.

❦ ❦

Index